All-in-One Bible Fun
Favorite Bible Stories
Preschool

Also available from Abingdon Press

All-in-One Bible Fun

Favorite Bible Stories
Elementary

Stories of Jesus
Preschool

Stories of Jesus
Elementary

Fruit of the Spirit
Preschool

Fruit of the Spirit
Elementary

Heroes of the Bible
Preschool

Heroes of the Bible
Elementary

Writer/Editor: Daphna Flegal
Production Editors: Billie Brownell, Anna Raitt
Production and Design Manager: Marcia C'deBaca
Illustrator: Robert S. Jones
Cover images: jupiterimages

All-in-One

BIBLE

FUN

Favorite Bible Stories
Preschool

ABINGDON PRESS
Nashville

All-in-One Bible Fun
Favorite Bible Stories
Preschool

09 10 11 12 13 14 15 16 17 18 - 10 9 8 7 6 5 4 3 2 1

MANUFACTURED IN THE UNITED STATES OF AMERICA

All-in-One BIBLE FUN Table of Contents

Bible Units in *Favorite Bible Stories*

Use these combinations if you choose to organize
the lessons in short-term units.

Favorite Old Testament Stories

Bible Story	Bible Verse
Jacob's Ladder	God said, "Remember, I will be with you." Genesis 28:15, GNT, adapted
Joseph	God said, "Remember, I will be with you." Genesis 28:15, GNT, adapted
Ruth	God said, "Remember, I will be with you." Genesis 28:15, GNT, adapted
Hannah and Samuel	As Samuel grew up, the LORD was with him. 1 Samuel 3:19
Samuel Listens	As Samuel grew up, the LORD was with him. 1 Samuel 3:19
David and Samuel	The LORD looks on the heart. 1 Samuel 16:7
David Plays the Harp	The LORD looks on the heart. 1 Samuel 16:7
David and Jonathan	A friend loves at all times. Proverbs 17:17

Favorite New Testament Stories

Bible Story	Bible Verse
The Two Houses	God is love. 1 John 4:8
The Sower	God is love. 1 John 4:8
The Good Samaritan	Love your neighbor as you love yourself. Luke 10:27, GNT
The Lost Sheep	God cares for you. 1 Peter 5:7, CEV
The Forgiving Father	God cares for you. 1 Peter 5:7, CEV

Supplies

(This is a comprehensive list of all the supplies needed if you choose to do all the activities. It is your choice whether your group will do all the activities.)

- Bible
- construction paper
- plain wrapping paper
- glue
- safety scissors, scissors
- clear plastic tape
- masking tape
- stapler, staples
- crayons or markers
- dark permanent marker
- colored cellophane
- six bean bags or sponge balls
- file folder
- magnetic strips, magnet
- measuring stick or measuring tape
- water, pitcher
- plastic table covering
- newspaper
- large paper grocery bags
- paper towels
- tempera paint
- paintbrushes, sponge paintbrushes
- watercolor paints
- shallow trays or box lids
- angel cookie cutters
- craft sticks
- paint smocks
- drinking straws
- packing peanuts

- plastic containers
- cotton balls, cotton swabs
- baby oil
- birdseed
- shallow tray or box lid
- first-aid kit supplies
- baskets
- dishpan or metal cake pan
- sponge
- flat rock
- hand-washing supplies
- rhythm instruments
- music CD and CD player
- seed packets
- box, box with lid
- sand

Welcome to *All-in-One Bible Fun*

Have fun learning favorite Bible stories! Each lesson in this teacher guide is filled with games and activities that will make learning fun for you and your children. Everything you need to teach is included in Abingdon's *All-in-One Bible Fun*, and with just a few additional supplies, your group can enjoy fun and enriching activities. Each lesson also has a box with a picture of a cookie,

We celebrate with joy because we know Jesus is alive!

that is repeated over and over again throughout the lesson. The cookie box states the Bible message in words your children will understand.

Use the following tips to help make *All-in-One Bible Fun* a success!

- Read through each lesson. Read the Bible passages.
- Memorize the Bible verse and the cookie box statement.
- Choose activities that fit your unique group of children and your time limitations. If time is limited, those activities we recommend are in **boldface** on the chart page and noted by a *balloon* beside each activity.

balloon symbol

- Practice telling the Bible story.
- Gather the supplies you will use for the lesson.
- Learn the music included in each lesson. All the songs are written to familiar tunes.
- Arrange your room space to fit the lesson. Move tables and chairs so there is plenty of room for the children to move and to sit on the floor.
- Copy the Reproducible pages for the lesson.

Preschoolers

Each child in your class is a one-of-a-kind child of God. Each child has his or her own name, background, family situation, and set of experiences. It is important to remember and celebrate the uniqueness of each child. Yet all of these one-of-a-kind children of God have some common needs.

- All children need love.
- All children need a sense of self-worth.
- All children need to feel a sense of accomplishment.
- All children need to have a safe place to be and to express their feelings.
- All children need to be surrounded by adults who love them.
- All children need to experience the love of God.

Preschoolers (children 3–5 years old) also have some common characteristics.

Their Bodies
- They do not sit still for very long.
- They have lots of energy.
- They enjoy moving (running, galloping, dancing, jumping, hopping).
- They are developing fine motor skills (learning to cut with scissors, learning to handle a ball, learning to tie their shoes).
- They enjoy using their senses (taste, touch, smell, hearing, seeing).

Their Minds
- They are learning more and more words.
- They enjoy music.
- They are learning to express their feelings.
- They like to laugh and be silly.
- They enjoy nonsense words.
- They are learning to identify colors, sizes, and shapes.
- They have an unclear understanding of time.
- They have a wonderful imagination.

Their Relationships
- They are beginning to interact with others as they play together.
- They are beginning to understand that other people have feelings.
- They are learning to wait for their turn.
- They can have a hard time leaving parents, especially their mother.
- They want to help.
- They love to feel important.

Their Hearts
- They need to handle the Bible and see others handle it.
- They need caring adults who model Christian attitudes and behaviors.
- They need to sing, move to, and say Bible verses.
- They need to hear clear, simple stories from the Bible.
- They can express simple prayers.
- They can experience wonder and awe at God's world.
- They can share food and money and make things for others.
- They can experience belonging at church.

All-in-One BIBLE FUN PRESCHOOL

Jacob's Ladder

Bible Verse

God said, "Remember, I will be with you."
Genesis 28:15, GNT, adapted

Bible Story

Genesis 28:10-17

Isaac and Rebekah had twin sons. The first was named Esau, a name referring to his hairy appearance; the second was named Jacob, a name referring to the fact that he came out of the womb holding his brother's heel. Esau became a hunter and his father's favorite, while Jacob's quiet nature was more appealing to Rebekah. The birth of the twins ensured that the promise made to Abraham would be fulfilled. Yet from the first, the promise was in jeopardy because of the conflicts between the two sons.

When Isaac believed himself to be near death, he asked Esau to prepare a meat stew for him. After he ate, Isaac planned to pass on to his firstborn the patriarchal blessing. But while Esau hunted for game for the stew, Rebekah convinced Jacob to disguise himself and to pretend to be his brother in order to obtain the blessing. Once given, the blessing could not be taken back. Esau was angry and planned to kill Jacob. When Rebekah heard of his plan, she insisted that

Jacob go away until his brother's anger had cooled. Under cover of seeking a wife from among his mother's people, Jacob left home.

When night came, Jacob lay his head upon a stone and slept. As he slept, he dreamed of angels of God ascending and descending a stairway or ladder between heaven and earth. At the top of the ladder God stood and spoke to Jacob.

Jacob's dream gave divine assurance and promise to the fearful, fleeing young man. God repeated the original promise made to Abraham and assured Jacob that all of the earth's inhabitants would be blessed through Jacob and his offspring. When Jacob awoke, he knew that he was in a holy place.

Young children learn about promises kept, and promises broken, from adults. Make every effort to keep the promises you give to the children you teach.

God is always with us.

If time is limited, we recommend those activities that are noted in **boldface**. Depending on your time and the number of children, you may be able to include more activities.

ACTIVITY	TIME	SUPPLIES	
Rock Pillows	10 minutes	**Plain paper, crayons, tape, stapler and staples, newspaper or other scrap paper**	JOIN THE FUN
Caravan Capers	5 minutes	Reproducible 1B (bottom)	BIBLE STORY FUN
Bible Story: Dream, Dream, Dream	10 minutes	**Reproducible 1A and 1B (top), tape or glue, file folder, scissors, magnetic strips, paper rocks from "Rock Pillows" activity**	
Bible Verse Fun	**5 minutes**	**Bible**	
Sing!	5 minutes	None	
Angel Antics	5 minutes	None	
Ladder Patter	10 minutes	Reproducible 1A, cotton balls, crayons, glue, tempera paint, shallow tray, paper towels, smocks, newspaper, angel cookie cutters	LIVE THE FUN
Ring-a-Round Prayers	**5 minutes**	**None**	

Rock Pillows

Say: Today our Bible story is about a man named Jacob. One day Jacob was going to another city. He traveled all day long. When it was night, Jacob stopped. He found a rock to use as a pillow and went to sleep. Let's make our paper into pretend rocks.

Give each child two pieces of plain paper. Show the children how to crumple the paper into balls and then smooth the papers flat again. Have the children repeat this process several times.

Say: Rocks are hard and rough. Feel the crumples you have made in your papers. *(Have the children run their fingers over their crumpled papers.)* **Let's pretend that the crumples are the rough edges of our rocks.**

Have the children place their papers flat on the table. Let the children color their papers with crayons. When each child has finished coloring, stack the two papers together, decorated sides out. Staple around three sides of the papers, leaving one side open.

Place a stack of newspaper or other scrap paper on the table or floor. Show the children how to tear off sheets of newspaper and crumple them into balls. Have the children stuff the newspaper balls into their pillows.

When each pillow is stuffed, staple the fourth side closed. Cover the prongs of the staples with strips of tape.

Say: While Jacob was sleeping, he had a dream. God spoke to Jacob in the dream. "God said, 'Remember, I will be with you'" (Genesis 28:15, GNT, adapted).

> ## God is always with us.

Have the children place their rock pillows in your story area.

Caravan Capers

Supplies

Reproducible
1B (bottom)

Say: Today our Bible story is about a man named Jacob. One day Jacob was going to another city. He traveled all day long. When people traveled in Bible times, sometimes they walked and sometimes they rode camels. Let's pretend that we are riding camels in a camel caravan.

Show the children the picture of the camel caravan (**Reproducible 1B, bottom**). Have the children pretend to ride camels and move about the room as you say the following movement poem. End the movement activity in your story area.

Let's pretend we're riding camels,
Traveling over desert sands.
(Pretend to ride camels;
hold reins and gallop around the room.)

Harump, harump.
Harump, harump.
(Stop; sway back and forth.)

Say goodbye to friends and family
On our way to far-off lands.
(Pretend to ride camels.)

Harump, harump.
Harump, harump.
(Stop; sway back and forth.)

Sitting on the humps of camels,
Bouncing as they dip and sway.
(Pretend to ride camels.)

Harump, harump.
Harump, harump.
(Stop; sway back and forth.)

God is with us as we travel.
God is with us every day.
(Pretend to ride camels.)

Harump, harump.
Harump, harump.
(Stop; sway back and forth.)

Dream, Dream, Dream

by Daphna Flegal

Photocopy the ladder (Reproducible 1A) *and the angels* (Reproducible 1B, top)*. Tape or glue the ladder onto a file folder. Cut a one-inch piece from a magnetic strip. Glue the strip onto the back of the angels. Place the file folder, angels, and a magnet nearby. Have the children stand next to their paper rocks from the "Rock Pillows" activity. Encourage the children to do the suggested motions.*

Say: Today our Bible story is about a man named Jacob. One day Jacob was going from his home to another city. He traveled all day long. When it was night, Jacob stopped. He found a rock to use as a pillow and went to sleep. Let's pretend that we are traveling with Jacob.

Jacob was tired. *(Take a deep breath and sigh.)* It had been a long day. He had walked and walked. *(Walk in place.)* Now the sun was going down. Soon it would be dark. Jacob knew it was time to stop and rest. *(Stop walking. Stretch arms and yawn.)* He was so tired; he was ready to go to sleep. *(Rub eyes.)* But Jacob was not near a house or an inn. He would have to sleep outside under the starry sky. Jacob stretched out on the ground. *(Sit down.)* He put a rock under his head to make a pillow. *(Encourage the children to put their heads on their paper rocks.)* Soon Jacob was asleep.

While Jacob was asleep, he had a dream. He dreamed that he saw a ladder. *(Hold up the file folder to show the children the ladder.)* The bottom of the ladder touched the ground. The top of the ladder went up into the sky. Angels of God were going up and down the ladder. *(Place the angels on the front of the ladder. Hold the magnet at the back of the file folder, catching the angels. Move the magnet up and down over the back of the file folder to move the angels up and down the ladder.)*

Jacob heard God's voice. "I am God. I give you this land. I promise that I will always be with you and your family. Remember, I will be with you."

Then Jacob woke up from his dream. *(Set the file folder aside.)*

"God was here, and I did not know it," said Jacob. "This place is special. From now on I will remember that God is always with me."

Hold the file folder with the ladder and angels. Call each child to come one at a time and use the magnet to move the angels up and down the ladder. Say the Bible verse for the child. Have the child repeat the verse after you.

Bible Verse Fun

Choose a child to hold the Bible open to Genesis 28:15.

Say: Today our Bible story is about a man named Jacob. One day Jacob was going to another city. He traveled all day long. When it was night, Jacob stopped. He found a rock to use as a pillow and went to sleep. While Jacob was sleeping, he had a dream. God spoke to Jacob in the dream. "God said, 'Remember, I will be with you'" (Genesis 28:15, GNT, adapted).

God is always with us.

Say the Bible verse, "God said, 'Remember, I will be with you'" (Genesis 28:15, GNT, adapted), for the children. Have the children say the Bible verse after you.

Help the children learn the Bible verse by singing. Sing the words printed below to the tune of "Mary Had a Little Lamb."

> "Remember, I will be with you,"
> "be with you, be with you."
> "Remember, I will be with you,"
> "I will be with you."

Play a game with the children to reinforce the Bible verse. Have each child take his or her rock pillow and place it on the floor in an open area of the room. Be sure that the pillows are placed far enough apart that the children will not bump into each other.

Say: Let's pretend that we are traveling with Jacob. When you hear me say, "Jacob, go to sleep," run to your pillow and lie down.

Say: Jacob, walk. *(Have the children walk around the room.)*

After a few minutes **say: Jacob, go to sleep.** *(Have the children run to their pillows and lie down.)*

Then **say: Jacob, wake up.** *(Have the children sit up.)*

While the children are sitting have them repeat the Bible verse with you: "God said, 'Remember, I will be with you'" (Genesis 28:15, GNT, adapted).

Continue the game, varying how you have the children move. Say things such as "Jacob, hop"; "Jacob, march"; "Jacob, gallop"; and "Jacob, crawl."

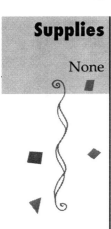

Supplies

None

Sing!

Sing the song "Jacob Had a Dream" to the tune of "The Farmer in the Dell." Encourage the children to do the suggested motions as you sing together.

Jacob Had a Dream
(Tune: "The Farmer in the Dell")

Oh, Jacob had a dream,
(Fold hands together on one side of your head.)
Oh, Jacob had a dream.
As he slept upon the ground,
(Touch the ground.)
Oh, Jacob had a dream.
(Fold hands together on one side of your head.)

Oh, Jacob had a dream,
(Fold hands on one side of your head.)
Oh, Jacob had a dream.
He saw a ladder reach to heav'n,
(Stretch arms up over your head.)
Oh, Jacob had a dream.
(Fold hands on one side of your head.)

Oh, Jacob had a dream,
(Fold hands on one side of your head.)
Oh, Jacob had a dream.

There were angels on the ladder,
(Wave your arms like angel's wings.)
Oh, Jacob had a dream.
(Fold hands on one side of your head.)

Oh, Jacob had a dream,
(Fold hands on one side of your head.)
Oh, Jacob had a dream.
God spoke to Jacob in the dream,
(Shake your index finger.)
Oh, Jacob had a dream.
(Fold hands on one side of your head.)

Oh, Jacob had a dream,
(Fold hands on one side of your head.)
Oh, Jacob had a dream.
God said, "I will be with you,"
(Point to self.)
Oh, Jacob had a dream.
(Fold hands on one side of your head.)

Words: Daphna Flegal © 2001 Abingdon Press.

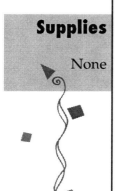

Supplies

None

Angel Antics

Enjoy using the following action verse with the children.

See the angels
(Flap arms like wings.)
Climb the ladder.
(Pretend to climb up ladder.)
Up and down,
(Stretch up, squat down.)
Up and down,
(Stretch up, squat down.)
Up and down they go.
(Stretch up, squat down.)

While Jacob's sleeping,
(Put hand under head as if sleeping.)
They climb the ladder.
(Pretend to climb up ladder.)
Up and down,
(Stretch up, squat down.)
Up and down,
(Stretch up, squat down.)
Up and down they go.
(Stretch up, squat down.)

Ladder Patter

Supplies

Reproducible 1A, cotton balls, crayons, glue, tempera paint, shallow tray, paper towels, smocks, newspaper, angel cookie cutters

Photocopy the ladder **(Reproducible 1A)** for each child. Cover the table with newspaper and have the children wear paint smocks. Place folded paper towels into a shallow tray. Pour tempera paint onto the paper towels to make a paint pad. Give each child a ladder. Let the children glue cotton balls at the top of the ladder to represent clouds. Let the children color around the bottom of the ladder to represent the ground. Let the children take turns pressing angel cookie cutters onto the paint pad and then onto their ladders.

Say: **While Jacob was sleeping, he had a dream. He saw a ladder that started on the ground and went up to the sky. Angels were going up and down the ladder. God spoke to Jacob in the dream. "God said, 'Remember, I will be with you'" (Genesis 28:15, GNT, adapted).**

God is always with us.

Ring-a-Round Prayers

Supplies

None

Have the children stand in a circle. Sing the song printed below to the tune of "Do You Know the Muffin Man?" Have the children walk around in the circle as you sing the first stanza.

Choose a child to stand in the center of the circle. Sing the second stanza of the song using the child's name. Then say the prayer for that child. Continue until each child has had an opportunity to stand in the middle and you have sung for each child. Encourage the children to sing with you.

> **Do you know that God is here,
> God is here, God is here?
> Do you know that God is here
> And with us all the time?**
>
> *(Child's name)* **knows that God is here,
> God is here, God is here.**
> *(Child's name)* **knows that God is here
> And with us all the time.**

Pray: **Thank you, God, for** *(child's name).* *(Child's name)* **will remember that you are always with us. Amen.**

REPRODUCIBLE 1A

ALL–IN–ONE BIBLE FUN

REPRODUCIBLE 1B

19

All-in-One
BIBLE PRESCHOOL
FUN

Joseph

Bible Verse

God said, "Remember, I will be with you."
Genesis 28:15, GNT, adapted

Bible Story

Genesis 37:1-36; 42:1–46:7

Joseph and his younger brother, Benjamin, were the only sons of Jacob's beloved wife, Rachel. Though Joseph became an important figure in biblical history, his early days clearly show that he had many faults and weaknesses. Perhaps because he was his father's favorite, he became a conceited tale-bearer and lorded it over his brothers. The familiar "coat of many colors" was more likely a long-sleeved garment that was a symbol of his privileged status, indicating that he stood above the necessity of manual labor. Laborers wore shorter garments with no sleeves that left their arms and legs free. The older brothers became angry and resentful, and only the action of one of them prevented Joseph's death.

God's plan for Joseph and for the remainder of Abraham's descendants was accomplished through Joseph's slavery and rise to power in Egypt as Pharaoh's chief minister.

In Egypt Joseph worked diligently, trusting God. God gave Joseph the ability to interpret dreams for the pharaoh, and through this ability Joseph was able to help Egypt survive a severe famine. This resulted in the pharaoh appointing Joseph to a position of power. Because of the famine in their homeland, Joseph's brothers arrived seeking food, and Joseph became reconciled with his family.

As we read the story today, we realize God's purpose in the events of Joseph's life—his dreams, his father's favoritism, and even his brothers' jealousy. Joseph remained faithful to God's promises and showed compassion and forgiveness to his brothers.

Jealousy is a natural part of childhood. When a child feels ignored or unloved, it is natural to act out those feelings. Our job is to help children discover their uniqueness and to let each child know that he or she is special.

God is always with us.

If time is limited, we recommend those activities that are noted in **boldface**. Depending on your time and the number of children, you may be able to include more activities.

ACTIVITY	TIME	SUPPLIES	
Rainbow Robes	10 minutes	Reproducible 2A, newspaper, paint smocks, watercolor paints, water, plastic containers, paint brushes	JOIN THE FUN
Color Shake	**10 minutes**	**Reproducible 2B; scissors; crayons; strips of red, blue, yellow, and green construction paper; glue, tape, or stapler and staples**	
Caravan Capers	5 minutes	Reproducible 1B (bottom)	BIBLE STORY FUN
Bible Story: The New Coat	**10 minutes**	**robe shakers (Reproducible 2B)**	
Bible Verse Fun	**5 minutes**	**Bible, Bible-times coat or an adult-size shirt**	
Bag It	10 minutes	paper grocery bags, scissors, crayons	
Sing!	5 minutes	paper bag coats from "Bag It" activity	
Joseph, Joseph	5 minutes	robe shakers from "Color Shake" activity (Reproducible 2B)	LIVE THE FUN
Ring-a-Round Prayers	**5 minutes**	**None**	

Supplies

Reproducible 2A, newspaper, paint smocks, watercolor paints, water, plastic containers, paint brushes

Rainbow Robes

Photocopy the robe **(Reproducible 2A)** for each child.

Say: Today our Bible story is about a young man named Joseph. Joseph's father loved Joseph very much. He gave Joseph a special robe. The robe had long sleeves and many colors. Let's paint Joseph's robe with beautiful colors.

Cover the table with newspaper. Have each child wear a paint smock to protect his or her clothing. Place containers of water and watercolor paints on the table for the children to share.

Give each child a paint brush and a robe picture. Show each child how to dip the brush into the water, rub the brush over the paint color and then onto his or her robe pictures. Encourage the children to make the robes colorful. Place the pictures flat to dry.

Supplies

Reproducible 2B; scissors; crayons; strips of red, blue, yellow, and green construction paper; glue, tape, or stapler and staples

Color Shake

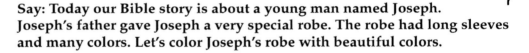

Photocopy the robe shakers **(Reproducible 2B)** for each child. Let the children decorate the robes with crayons. Show the children how to fold the robes along the dotted lines.

Say: Today our Bible story is about a young man named Joseph. Joseph's father gave Joseph a very special robe. The robe had long sleeves and many colors. Let's color Joseph's robe with beautiful colors.

While the children are coloring, prepare strips of colored construction paper. Cut one-inch strips from red, blue, yellow, and green construction paper. Make enough strips of each color so that there will be at least two shakers of the same color. If you do not have one of these colors, substitute a different color and then substitute that color in the story. Help the children identify the colors, and let the children choose one color. Help the children glue, tape, or staple three or four of the same color strips to the bottom of their robes. Glue or staple the bottom of the robes together over the strips. Each child should have only one color of strips.

Say: These colors might have been in Joseph's beautiful robe.

Show the children how to hold the robe part of their shakers. Practice shaking the colors with the children. Call out a color, and have all the children with that color of shaker wave their shakers back and forth. Have the children place their shakers in the story area.

Caravan Capers

Supplies

Reproducible
1B (bottom)

Say: Today our Bible story is about a young man named Joseph. In our story Joseph travels to another country called Egypt. When people traveled in Bible times, sometimes they walked and sometimes they rode camels. Let's pretend that we are riding camels in a camel caravan.

Show the children the picture of the camel caravan **(Reproducible 1B, bottom)**. Have the children pretend to ride camels and move about the room as you say the following movement poem. End the movement activity in your story area.

Let's pretend we're riding camels,
Traveling over desert sands.
*(Pretend to ride camels;
hold reins and gallop around the room.)*

Harump, harump.
Harump, harump.
(Stop; sway back and forth.)

Say goodbye to friends and family
On our way to far-off lands.
(Pretend to ride camels.)

Harump, harump.
Harump, harump.
(Stop; sway back and forth.)

Sitting on the humps of camels,
Bouncing as they dip and sway.
(Pretend to ride camels.)

Harump, harump.
Harump, harump.
(Stop; sway back and forth.)

God is with us as we travel.
God is with us every day.
(Pretend to ride camels.)

Harump, harump.
Harump, harump.
(Stop; sway back and forth.)

God is always with us.

The New Coat

by Daphna Flegal

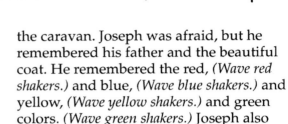

Have the children hold their robe shakers (Reproducible 2B) as you tell the story. Each time you name a color, have the children with that color shaker hold up the shaker and wave it in the air.

"Look at my new coat!" Joseph called to his brothers. He held out his arms in the long sleeves of his coat and turned around. "It has so many beautiful colors," he said. "It has red, *(Wave red shakers.)* and blue, *(Wave blue shakers.)* and yellow, *(Wave yellow shakers.)* and green colors." *(Wave green shakers.)*

"Where did you get that coat?" asked one of Joseph's brothers.

"Father gave it to me," answered Joseph.

The brothers were not happy about Joseph's coat. They did not like the beautiful colors. They did not like the red, *(Wave red shakers.)* and blue, *(Wave blue shakers.)* and yellow, *(Wave yellow shakers.)* and green colors. *(Wave green shakers.)*

"Father has never given any of us a coat like that," said one brother.

"Father loves Joseph more than he loves us," said another brother.

The brothers decided to do something unkind to Joseph. They tore Joseph's coat with its beautiful colors. Then they pushed Joseph into a big hole.

"Look," said one brother. "Do you see that caravan? It's on its way to Egypt." "Let's sell Joseph to the caravan," said another brother. "They will take him far away to Egypt."

The brothers pulled Joseph out of the hole. Soon Joseph was on his way to Egypt with the caravan. Joseph was afraid, but he remembered his father and the beautiful coat. He remembered the red, *(Wave red shakers.)* and blue, *(Wave blue shakers.)* and yellow, *(Wave yellow shakers.)* and green colors. *(Wave green shakers.)* Joseph also remembered that God was with him.

When Joseph got to Egypt, he had many adventures. He became an important man in Egypt. One day Joseph's brothers came to Egypt to buy food. The brothers had to buy the food from Joseph. When Joseph saw his brothers, he remembered his beautiful coat. He remembered the red, *(Wave red shakers.)* and blue, *(Wave blue shakers.)* and yellow, *(Wave yellow shakers.)* and green colors. *(Wave green shakers.)* Joseph also remembered that God was with him.

At first the brothers did not know Joseph because he had grown up and had become an important man. When Joseph told the brothers who he was, they told Joseph that they were sorry that they had been unkind to him. Joseph forgave his brothers.

"God is with me," said Joseph. "I'm glad that I came to live in Egypt."

He gave his brothers the food they needed. Joseph's brothers and Joseph's father came to Egypt to live with Joseph. Joseph was happy to see his father again. He remembered the beautiful coat his father had given him. The coat with the red, *(Wave red shakers.)* and blue, *(Wave blue shakers.)* and yellow, *(Wave yellow shakers.)* and green colors. *(Wave green shakers.)* Joseph also remembered that God was with him.

Bible Verse Fun

Choose a child to hold the Bible open to Genesis 28:15.

Say: Today our Bible story is about a young man named Joseph. Joseph grew up to be an important man. He had many adventures, some good and some bad. Joseph always remembered that God was with him.

God is always with us.

Say the Bible verse, "God said, 'Remember, I will be with you'" (Genesis 28:15, GNT, adapted), for the children. Have the children say the Bible verse after you.

Help the children learn the Bible verse by singing. Sing the words printed below to the tune of "Mary Had a Little Lamb."

> "Remember, I will be with you,"
> "be with you, be with you."
> "Remember, I will be with you,"
> "I will be with you."

Play a game with the children to reinforce the Bible verse.

Say: Joseph had a special coat. Let's play a game with a coat.

Show the children a Bible-times coat or an adult-size shirt. The coat or shirt needs to open in the front and not be too long for the children. Set the coat on a chair on one side of the room. Have the children line up on the opposite side of the room.

Have the first child in line hop to the coat, stop, put on the coat, and say the Bible verse: "God said, 'Remember, I will be with you'" (Genesis 28:15, GNT, adapted). Then have the child hop back to the line. This child will take off the coat, give it to the next child, and then go to the end of the line.

The next child will put on the coat, hop to the chair, say the Bible verse, and hop back again. This child will take off the coat, give it to the next child, and go to the end of the line. Continue until every child has a turn.

If time permits, continue the game, changing how the children move (march, tiptoe, take baby steps, and so forth).

Supplies

paper grocery bags, scissors, crayons

Bag It

Cut a paper bag into a coat for each child. If the bags have printing on them, turn them inside out. Turn the bag upside down. Cut a slit up the middle of one side. At the top of the slit, continue to cut and form a circular space for the neck. Cut holes for the arms on the two narrow sides of the bag.

Say: Today our Bible story is about Joseph and a very special robe. The robe had long sleeves and many colors. Let's make Joseph's robe.

Encourage the children to decorate the paper bag robes with many colors of crayons. Help the children put on their robes.

Say: God was with Joseph. God is always with us.

Supplies

paper bag coats from "Bag It" activity

Sing!

Sing the song printed below to the tune of "The Farmer in the Dell." Have the children wear their paper coats from the "Bag It" activity and do the motions.

Joseph Had a Coat
(Tune: "The Farmer in the Dell")

O Joseph had a coat
O Joseph had a coat.
(Hold edges of coat.)
The coat had many colors,
(Hold out arms, turn around.)
O Joseph had a coat.
(Hold edges of coat.)

His brothers, they were mad.
His brothers, they were mad.
(Put hands on hips; stomp feet.)
Because of Joseph's special coat,
(Hold out arms, turn around.)
His brothers, they were mad.
(Put hands on hips; stomp feet.)

To Egypt Joseph went.
To Egypt Joseph went.
(March in place.)
The Lord was with young Joseph.
(Hold out arms, turn around.)
To Egypt Joseph went.
(March in place.)

O Joseph helped the king.
O Joseph helped the king.
(Bow from waist.)
King Pharaoh asked for Joseph's help,
(Hold out arms, turn around.)
O Joseph helped the king.
(Bow from waist.)

O Joseph shared the food.
O Joseph shared the food.
(Pretend to eat.)
His brothers came to buy some food,
(Hold out arms, turn around.)
O Joseph shared the food.
(Pretend to eat.)

His brothers Joseph loved.
His brothers Joseph loved.
(Hug self.)
They brought their father to Egypt.
(Hold out arms, turn around.)
His brothers Joseph loved.
(Hug self.)

Joseph, Joseph

Supplies

robe shakers from "Color Shakes" activity (Reproducible 2B)

Choose one child to be Joseph. Have the children hold their robe shakers and stand in a circle with Joseph in the middle. Say the chant printed below.

> **Joseph, Joseph,**
> **What's that color?**
> **What's that color**
> **On your coat?**

Then shout out a color such as: "It's red!" Have all the children holding red robe shakers change places in the circle. Have Joseph try to get to one of the places in the circle before the switch is complete. The child left without a place in the circle becomes the next Joseph. Have the new Joseph stand in the middle of the circle and repeat the chant.

Continue the game, choosing different colors to switch places. Every once in a while, shout "All colors run!" and have everyone switch places.

Ring-a-Round Prayers

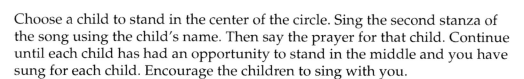

Supplies

None

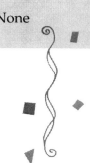

Have the children stand in a circle. Sing the song printed below to the tune of "Do You Know the Muffin Man?" Have the children walk around in the circle as you sing the first stanza.

Choose a child to stand in the center of the circle. Sing the second stanza of the song using the child's name. Then say the prayer for that child. Continue until each child has had an opportunity to stand in the middle and you have sung for each child. Encourage the children to sing with you.

> **Do you know that God is here,**
> **God is here, God is here?**
> **Do you know that God is here**
> **And with us all the time?**
>
> (*Child's name*) **knows that God is here,**
> **God is here, God is here.**
> (*Child's name*) **knows that God is here**
> **And with us all the time.**

Pray: Thank you, God, for (*child's name*). (*Child's name*) **will remember that you are always with us. Amen.**

REPRODUCIBLE 2A

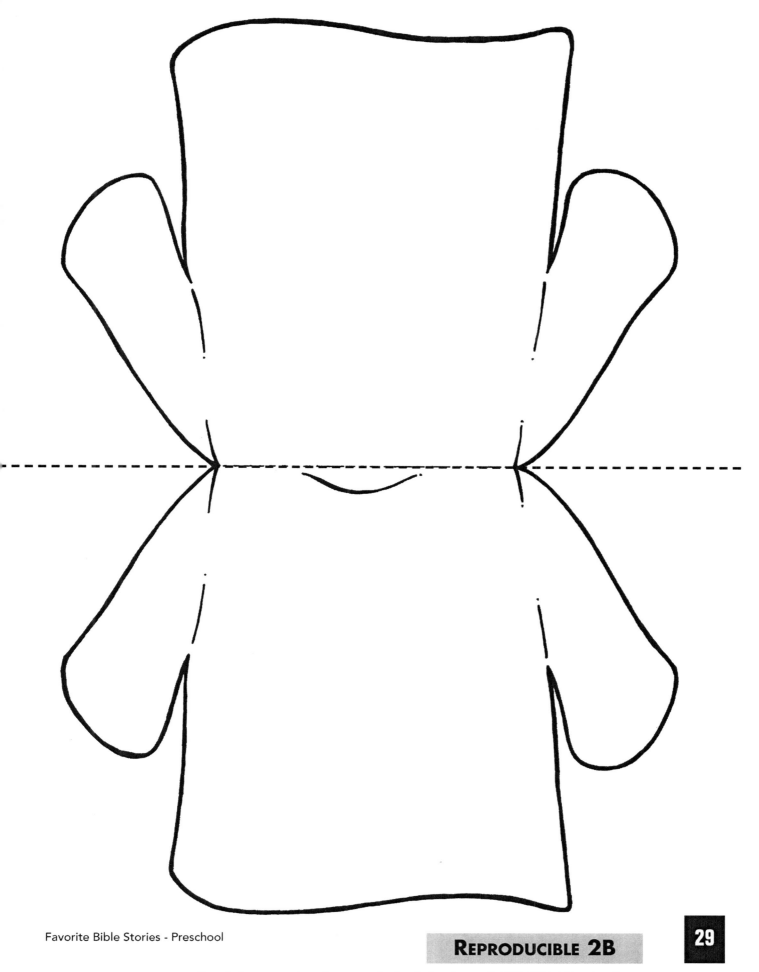

REPRODUCIBLE 2B

29

Ruth

Bible Verse

God said, "Remember, I will be with you."
Genesis 28:15, GNT, adapted

Bible Story

The Book of Ruth

The Book of Ruth is a story of love and concern within one family and how that family grew to include outsiders. During this time in Israel's history it proved an allegory of how Israel should relate to foreigners.

Elimelech and Naomi, along with their two sons, had joined others in Moab seeking refuge from the famine in their homeland. There the sons married Moab women, but soon all the men died. Naomi heard that God had provided food for God's people and determined to go back to Bethlehem. She encouraged both of her daughters-in-law to return to their fathers' houses.

Orpah tearfully followed Naomi's advice, but Ruth begged to be allowed to go with Naomi and help care for her. Both women were filled with self-giving love: Naomi was willing to let Ruth return home, and Ruth was willing to remain with Naomi. Ruth and Naomi are examples of how God acts

through ordinary people when ordinary people live in the image of God.

Leaders of the Jewish community encouraged Jews returning to their homeland to send their foreign wives or husbands back to the lands from whence they came. So the Book of Ruth can be seen as subtle propaganda against the need for purity of blood lines. Obed, the child of a mixed marriage between Ruth and Boaz, was the grandfather of King David, Israel's greatest king.

The situation of Ruth and Naomi, alone and yet still a family, is very relevant to today's families, which come in many different configurations. Children from homes with one parent particularly may identify with Ruth and Naomi's situation. It is important for all children to know that it is love and caring that make families out of groups of people.

God is always with us.

If time is limited, we recommend those activities that are noted in **boldface**. Depending on your time and the number of children, you may be able to include more activities.

ACTIVITY	TIME	SUPPLIES	
Harvest Hunt	**5 minutes**	**Reproducible 3A, scissors, basket**	JOIN THE FUN
Pass-It Basket	10 minutes	Reproducible 3A, two baskets	
Caravan Capers	5 minutes	Reproducible 1B (bottom)	BIBLE STORY FUN
Bible Story: Come and Go	**10 minutes**	**None**	
Bible Verse Fun	**5 minutes**	**Bible**	
Sing!	5 minutes	None	
Picture This	10 minutes	Reproducible 3A, newspaper, crayons, cotton balls, baby oil; or, cotton swabs, birdseed, glue, shallow tray or box lid	
Grain Chain	10 minutes	Reproducible 3B, scissors, crayon or marker, glue or tape, optional: construction paper strips	LIVE THE FUN
Ring-a-Round Prayers	**5 minutes**	**None**	

Supplies

Reproducible 3A, scissors, baskets

Harvest Hunt

Photocopy the grain picture **(Reproducible 3A)** for each child. Cut out the picture around the oval. Hide the grain pictures around the room. Place a basket on the rug or on a table. Greet the children as they enter the room.

Say: Today our Bible story is about a woman named Ruth. Ruth was kind to her mother-in-law, Naomi. Ruth left her home and went with Naomi to a town called Bethlehem. When they got to Bethlehem, Ruth went to the fields to find grain so that she and Naomi would be able to make bread to eat. Look around the room. Find a picture of a stalk of grain and bring the picture back to the basket.

Have each child find one grain picture and put in in the basket.

Say: God was with Ruth. God was with her when she left her home and moved to Bethlehem with Naomi. God was with Ruth when she picked the grain so that she and Naomi would be able to make bread to eat.

God is always with us.

Supplies

Reproducible 3A, two baskets

Pass-It Basket

Photcopy and cut out a grain picture **(Reproducible 3A)** for each child. Or use the grain pictures from the "Harvest Hunt" activity. Place the pictures in one of the baskets.

Have the children stand in a row. Give the first child in the row the basket with the grain pictures. Give the last child in the row an empty basket.

Say: Today our Bible story is about a woman named Ruth. Ruth was kind to her mother-in-law, Naomi. She left her home and went with Naomi to a town called Bethlehem. When they got to Bethlehem, Ruth went to the fields to find grain so that she and Naomi could make bread to eat. Let's help Ruth pick the grain and take it home to Naomi.

Say the word "Go!" Have the first child pull a grain picture out of the basket and pass it along the row to the last child. Have the last child put the picture in the empty basket. Continue until all the grain pictures have been passed down the row. If time permits, have the child at the end of the row bring the basket with the grain pictures to the beginning of the row. Give the empty basket to the new child at the end of the row. Say, "Go!" and pass the grain again.

Caravan Capers

Supplies

Reproducible
1B (bottom)

Say: Today our Bible story is about a woman named Ruth. Ruth left her home and went with Naomi to a town called Bethlehem. When people traveled in Bible times, sometimes they walked and sometimes they rode camels. Let's pretend that we are riding camels in a camel caravan.

Show the children the picture of the camel caravan **(Reproducible 1B, bottom)**. Have the children pretend to ride camels and move about the room as you say the following movement poem. End the movement activity in your story area.

Let's pretend we're riding camels,
Traveling over desert sands.
(Pretend to ride camels;
hold reins and gallop around the room.)

Harump, harump.
Harump, harump.
(Stop; sway back and forth.)

Say goodbye to friends and family
On our way to far-off lands.
(Pretend to ride camels.)

Harump, harump.
Harump, harump.
(Stop; sway back and forth.)

Sitting on the humps of camels,
Bouncing as they dip and sway.
(Pretend to ride camels.)

Harump, harump.
Harump, harump.
(Stop; sway back and forth.)

God is with us as we travel.
God is with us every day.
(Pretend to ride camels.)

Harump, harump.
Harump, harump.
(Stop; sway back and forth.)

Come and Go

by Daphna Flegal

Have the children stand in a circle as you tell the story. Have the children say the refrain and do the motions with you each time the refrain appears in the story.

Naomi and her husband had two sons. They lived in a town called Bethlehem. The land in Bethlehem became very dry. Naomi and her husband could not grow food to eat. They decided to move to another town, far away from Bethlehem. God was with Naomi and her family in Bethlehem. God was with Naomi and her family as they moved to a new place.

Come and go with Naomi. *(Wave "come here.")*
God will be with us. *(Cross hands over heart.)*
Come and go with Naomi. *(Wave "come here.")*
Let's walk! *(Walk in place.)*

Naomi and her family were happy in their new home. Naomi's two sons married two women who lived in the new town. The women were named Ruth and Orpah. Naomi's husband died. Then Naomi's two sons died. Naomi was very sad. God was with Naomi when she was happy. God was with Naomi when she was sad.

Come and go with Naomi. *(Wave "come here.")*
God will be with us. *(Cross hands over heart.)*
Come and go with Naomi. *(Wave "come here.")*
Let's cry! *(Rub eyes.)*

Naomi told Ruth and Orpah that she was going back to Bethlehem. Orpah decided to stay in the new land, but Ruth wanted to go with Naomi. God was with Orpah as she stayed in the new land. God was with Ruth and Naomi as they traveled back to Naomi's home in Bethlehem.

Come and go with Ruth. *(Wave "come here.")*
God will be with us. *(Cross hands over heart.)*
Come and go with Ruth. *(Wave "come here.")*
Let's walk! *(Walk in place.)*

Ruth and Naomi took care of each other. When they needed food to eat, Ruth went to the field to pick up the grain that the workers left on the ground. Ruth and Naomi used the grain to make bread. God was with Ruth and Naomi as they took care of each other.

Come and go with Ruth. *(Wave "come here.")*
God will be with us. *(Cross hands over heart.)*
Come and go with Ruth. *(Wave "come here.")*
Let's pick grain! *(Bend over; pretend to pick up grain.)*

While Ruth picked the grain, she met a kind man named Boaz. Boaz and Ruth fell in love and got married. Soon Ruth had a baby. Naomi was very happy about the baby. She was happy about her new family. God was with Naomi and Ruth and their new family.

Come and go with Ruth. *(Wave "come here.")*
God will be with us. *(Cross hands over heart.)*
Come and go with Ruth. *(Wave "come here.")*
Let's rock the baby! *(Pretend to rock a baby.)*

Bible Verse Fun

Choose a child to hold the Bible open to Genesis 28:15.

Say: Today our Bible story is about a woman named Ruth. Ruth left her home and went with her mother-in-law, Naomi, to a town called Bethlehem. When they got to Bethlehem, Ruth went to the fields to find grain so that she and Naomi would be able to make bread to eat. While she was picking grain, Ruth met a kind man named Boaz. Ruth and Boaz got married. God was with Ruth and Naomi and Boaz.

> ## God is always with us.

Say the Bible verse, "God said, 'Remember, I will be with you'" (Genesis 28:15, GNT, adapted), for the children. Have the children say the Bible verse after you.

Help the children learn the Bible verse by singing. Sing the words printed below to the tune of "Mary Had a Little Lamb."

> "Remember, I will be with you,"
> "be with you, be with you."
> "Remember, I will be with you,"
> "I will be with you."

Play a game with the children to reinforce the Bible verse. This game is like "Mother, May I?" Invite the children to an open area of the room.

Say: Ruth and Boaz and Naomi were a family. Ruth and Boaz had a baby named Obed. Naomi was baby Obed's grandmother. Let's play a game called "Grandmother, May I?" I will pretend to be the grandmother.

Stand in front of the playing area. Have the children go to the back.

Tell the children different ways to move forward, like "take three baby steps," "crawl like a baby until I say stop," or "take one giant step." Tell the children to ask, "Grandmother, may I?" and then move forward.

Let the children enjoy moving. When the children reach you, give each child a hug and say the Bible verse: "God said, 'Remember, I will be with you'" (Genesis 28:15, GNT, adapted).

Do not make the game a competition. Play as long as the children continue to show interest.

Supplies

None

Sing!

Say: Ruth went to the fields to find grain so that she and Naomi would be able to make bread to eat. One kind of grain that grew in Bible times was barley. Let's pretend that we are Ruth, picking up barley.

Have the children move to an open area of the room. Sing the words printed below to the tune of "Pickin' Up Paw Paws." Have the children do the motions as they sing. Repeat the song several times.

Pickin' Up Barley
(Tune: "Pickin' Up Paw Paws")

Pickin' up barley
(Pretend to pick up grain from the ground.)
And puttin' it in the basket.
(Hold one arm in a circle to make a pretend basket. Pretend to put grain in the basket.)
Pickin' up barley
(Pretend to pick up grain.)

And puttin' it in the basket.
(Pretend to put grain in a basket.)
Pickin' up barley
(Pretend to pick up grain.)
And puttin' it in the basket.
(Pretend to put grain in a basket.)
Way down yonder in the barley field.

Supplies

Reproducible 3A, newspaper, crayons, cotton balls, baby oil; or, cotton swabs, birdseed, glue, shallow tray or box lid

Picture This

Photocopy the grain picture **(Reproducible 3A)** for each child. Give each child a picture. Let the children make stained-glass windows or seed mosaics with their pictures.

Stained-glass windows. Cover the work area with newspaper. Let the children color the pictures with crayons. Have the children turn the pictures over. Pour a small amount of baby oil on a cotton ball. Show the children how to rub the oil over the backs of their pictures. Hold the pictures up to the light. The oil will make the pictures translucent.

Seed mosaics. Have the children use cotton swabs to brush glue onto their pictures. Place each picture in a shallow tray or box lid. Show the children how to sprinkle birdseed over the glue. Shake off the excess seeds.

Say: Today our Bible story is about a woman named Ruth. Ruth was kind to her mother-in-law, Naomi. Ruth left her home and went with Naomi to a town called Bethlehem. When they got to Bethlehem, Ruth went to the fields to find grain so that she and Naomi would be able to make bread to eat. While Ruth was picking up the grain, she met a kind man named Boaz. Ruth and Boaz got married. God was with Ruth and Naomi and Boaz. God is always with us.

Grain Chain

Supplies

Reproducible 3B, scissors, crayon or marker, glue or tape, optional: construction paper strips

Photocopy and cut out the grain chain strips **(Reproducible 3B)**. Make sure you have at least one chain for each child. Write each child's name on a grain chain. If you have older children, let them write their names themselves.

Show the children how to link the strips together with glue or tape to form one chain. Add construction paper links if you want to make the chain longer.

Say: Ruth was kind to her mother-in-law, Naomi. Ruth left her home and went with Naomi to a town called Bethlehem. When they got to Bethlehem, Ruth went to the fields to find grain so that she and Naomi would be able to make bread to eat. While Ruth was picking up the grain, she met a kind man named Boaz. Ruth and Boaz got married. God was with Ruth and Naomi and Boaz. God is always with us. God is with *(child's name)*. *(Touch each link on the grain chain as you say the child's name.)*

God is always with us.

Ring-a-Round Prayers

Supplies

None

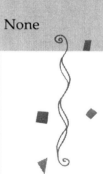

Have the children stand in a circle. Sing the song printed below to the tune of "Do You Know the Muffin Man?" Have the children walk around in the circle as you sing the first stanza.

Choose a child to stand in the center of the circle. Sing the second stanza of the song using the child's name. Then say the prayer for that child. Continue until each child has had an opportunity to stand in the middle and you have sung for each child. Encourage the children to sing with you.

Do you know that God is here,
God is here, God is here?
Do you know that God is here
And with us all the time?

(Child's name) knows that God is here,
God is here, God is here.
(Child's name) knows that God is here
And with us all the time.

Pray: Thank you, God, for *(child's name)*. *(Child's name)* will remember that you are always with us. Amen.

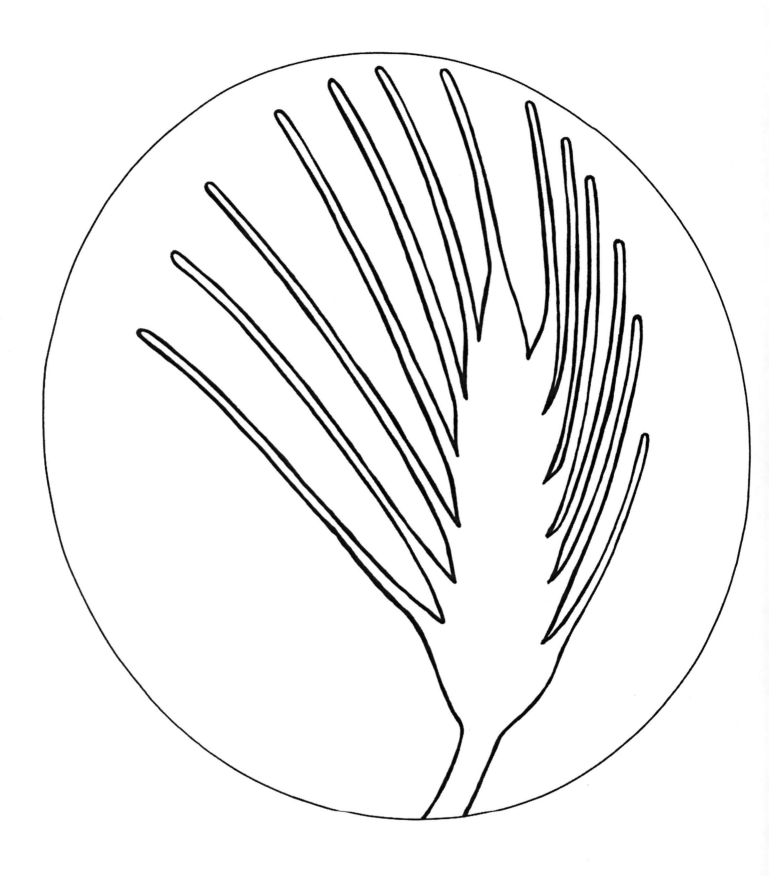

REPRODUCIBLE 3A

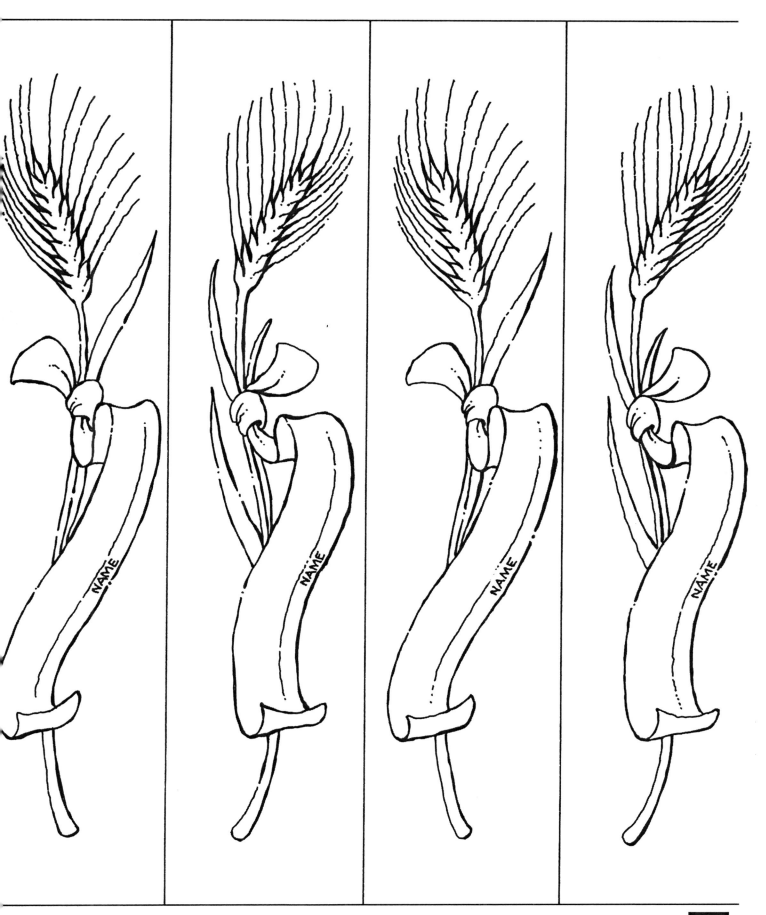

REPRODUCIBLE 3B

Hannah and Samuel

Bible Verse

As Samuel grew up, the LORD was with him.

1 Samuel 3:19

Bible Story

1 Samuel 1:1-28

The Book of Samuel begins with the story of Elkanah and his wife Hannah. Hannah was barren. At this time in biblical culture a married woman who had not borne children was a source of scorn. Elkanah had sons by his other wife, Peninnah, and Peninnah made fun of Hannah. Yet Elkanah loved Hannah and tried in other ways to compensate for her lack of children.

Hannah was a woman of faith. She prayed for a son and promised to dedicate her child to God. God answered her prayers when she gave birth to a son whom she named Samuel, whose name means "asked of God."

Hannah nurtured Samuel until he was weaned, which was at about three years of age, according to the culture of the day. Then she fulfilled her promise to God and joyfully dedicated her son to the Lord.

For Hannah this dedication meant that Samuel had been set apart from others for the special purpose of serving God. She vowed that Samuel would live a holy consecrated life as a Nazirite and a minister in the temple. Being a Nazirite meant that Samuel was dedicated to lifelong service to God.

Preschoolers may have difficulty with the story of Hannah leaving Samuel at the temple. They may be afraid that their parents will leave them at church. Emphasize Hannah's love for Samuel and her joy at his birth, rather than her decision to leave him at the temple.

Talk to your children about prayer. Help them understand that prayer is not magical. God answers all prayers, but not always in the way we expect.

God is with us as we grow.

If time is limited, we recommend those activities that are noted in **boldface**. Depending on your time and the number of children, you may be able to include more activities.

ACTIVITY	TIME	SUPPLIES	
Growin' Up	**15 minutes**	**Reproducibles 4A and 4B, scissors, masking tape, crayons or markers, measuring stick or tape**	**JOIN THE FUN**
Practice a New Skill	10 minutes	safety scissors (right- and left-handed), scrap paper	
Hannah's Hop	5 minutes	None	**BIBLE STORY FUN**
Bible Story: Hannah Had a Son	**10 minutes**	**None**	
Bible Verse Fun	**5 minutes**	**Bible, masking tape**	
Growing With God	10 minutes	None	
Shout a Verse	5 minutes	None	**LIVE THE FUN**
Whisper a Prayer	**5 minutes**	**None**	

Growin' Up

Photocopy and cut out the growth chart **(Reproducible 4A)**. Photocopy the "Look at Me" poster **(Reproducible 4B)** for each child. Use a measuring stick or tape to measure two feet from the floor. Use masking tape to mount the chart on a wall or door at the 2-foot mark. Greet each child as he or she enters the room.

Say: Today our Bible story is about a woman named Hannah. Hannah wanted a baby. She prayed to God, and God answered her prayer. Hannah had a baby boy. She named her baby Samuel. Samuel grew and grew, just like you grow and grow. God was with Samuel as he grew.

> ## God is with us as we grow.

Use the growth chart to measure each child's height. Write each child's name on a poster. Fill in the child's age in the space provided. Mark the child's height in the space provided.

Give each child his or her poster. Let the children decorate the posters with crayons or markers. Display the posters around your room.

Practice a New Skill

Let the children practice cutting scraps of paper with safety scissors. Make sure the children know safety rules for using scissors:
- Use scissors only at the table.
- You must stay seated while you are cutting with scissors.
- Scissors are only used for cutting paper.
- If you hand a pair of scissors to someone else, wrap your fist around the pointed end and let the other person grasp the handles.
- Carefully put the scissors away when you are finished.

Show the children how to hold the scissors. Some children will be more skilled at cutting than others. Learning to cut is a great achievement for young children. Affirm all the children as they try to cut.

Say: When you were a baby, you were not allowed to have scissors. Now that you are growing, you can practice cutting with scissors. I'm glad each one of you is growing. God is with us as we grow.

Encourage the children to pick up any paper scraps.

Hannah's Hop

Supplies

None

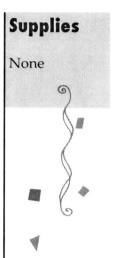

Say: Our Bible story is about Hannah. Hannah wanted a baby. She prayed to God, and God answered her prayer. Hannah had a baby boy. She named her baby Samuel. Samuel grew and grew. God was with Samuel as he grew.

Lead the children in hopping around the room as you say the following action poem for your children. End the hopping in your story area.

Hannah went to the temple
To talk to God in prayer.

So let's hop, hop here,
(Hop twice on one foot.)
And hop, hop there,
(Hop twice on the other foot.)
And hop, hop everywhere.
(Hop twice on both feet.)

She asked God for a baby boy
'Cause she knew God answered prayer.

So let's hop, hop here,
(Hop twice on one foot.)
And hop, hop there,
(Hop twice on the other foot.)
And hop, hop everywhere.
(Hop twice on both feet.)

Soon she had baby Samuel.
He was the answer to her prayer.

So let's hop, hop here,
(Hop twice on one foot.)
And hop, hop there,
(Hop twice on the other foot.)
And hop, hop everywhere.
(Hop twice on both feet.)

God was with Samuel as he grew.
Hannah thanked God with a prayer.

So let's hop, hop here,
(Hop twice on one foot.)
And hop, hop there,
(Hop twice on the other foot.)
And hop, hop everywhere.
(Hop twice on both feet.)

Hannah Had a Son

by Daphna Flegal

Say: Today our Bible story is about a woman named Hannah. Hannah wanted a baby. She prayed to God, and God answered her prayer. I need your help telling the story about Hannah. I will tell part of the story, and then I will sing a song. I want you to sing the song with me.

Tell the story to the children. Sing the stanzas to the tune of "The Farmer in the Dell"and do the suggested motions. Encourage the children to sing and move with you.

Hannah had no children, and she wanted a baby very much. She went to the temple to pray to God.

"O God," prayed Hannah, "I want a baby boy to love."

Sing
O Hannah prayed to God.
(Fold hands in prayer.)
O Hannah prayed to God.
She prayed that she would have a son.
O Hannah prayed to God.

Soon Hannah had a baby boy.
Hannah's baby was named Samuel.

Sing
O Hannah had a son.
(Pretend to rock baby.)
O Hannah had a son,
She had a son named Sam-u-el,
O Hannah had a son.

Samuel grew and grew and grew. As Samuel grew up, the Lord was with him.

Sing
O Samuel grew and grew.
(Crouch down and slowly stand with arms above head.)
O Samuel grew and grew.
From tiny baby to great big boy,
O Samuel grew and grew.

As Samuel grew up, he served God.

Sing
O Samuel grew and grew.
(Crouch down and slowly stand with arms above head.)
O Samuel grew and grew.
As he grew, he served the Lord.
O Samuel grew and grew.

Bible Verse Fun

Choose a child to hold the Bible open to 1 Samuel 3:19.

Say: Today our Bible story is about a woman named Hannah. Hannah wanted a baby. She prayed to God, and God answered her prayer. Hannah had a baby boy. She named her baby Samuel. Samuel grew and grew. God was with Samuel as he grew.

God is with us as we grow.

Say the Bible verse, "As Samuel grew up, the LORD was with him" (1 Samuel 3:19), for the children. Have the children say the Bible verse after you.

Help the children learn the Bible verse by singing. Sing the words printed below to the tune of "The Farmer in the Dell." Clap in rhythm to the tune on the fourth line.

As Samuel grew up,
As Samuel grew up,
the LORD was with him,
(clap, clap, clap.)
As Samuel grew up.

Play a game with the children to reinforce the Bible verse. Have the children move to one side of the room. Use masking tape to make a goal line on the other side of the room.

Say: Our Bible story is about a woman named Hannah. Hannah wanted a baby. She prayed to God, and God answered her prayer. Hannah had a baby boy. She named her baby Samuel. Samuel grew and grew, just like you grow and grow. When you were a baby just learning to walk, you had to take baby steps. Now that you have grown bigger, you can take giant steps.

Have the children take baby steps toward the taped line.

After a few seconds, **say: Stop!**

Say the Bible verse with the children: "As Samuel grew up, the LORD was with him" (1 Samuel 3:19).

Then have the children take giant steps toward the taped line. Continue stopping, saying the Bible verse, and stepping with baby or giant steps until all the children reach the taped line.

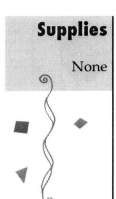

Supplies

None

Growing With God

Have the children move to an open area of the room.

Say: Today our Bible story is about a woman named Hannah. Hannah wanted a baby. She prayed to God, and God answered her prayer. Hannah had a baby boy. She named her baby Samuel. Samuel grew and grew. God was with Samuel as he grew.

God is with us as we grow.

Say the following statements for the children and have the children do the motions. Give the children a few minutes to move around the room after each statement. Then have the children stop wherever they are in the room. Say, "God is with us as we grow" and do the motion. Continue with the next statement and motion.

God is with us when we are babies. Let's crawl like babies.
(Crawl around the room.)

Stop!
God is with us as we grow!
(Crouch down and slowly stand with arms above head.)

God is with us when we take our first steps. Let's walk with baby steps.
(Take baby steps around the room.)

Stop!
God is with us as we grow!
(Crouch down and slowly stand with arms above head.)

God is with us when we grow big enough to march. Let's march.
(March around the room.)

Stop!
God is with us as we grow!
(Crouch down and slowly stand with arms above head.)

God is with us when we grow big enough to gallop. Let's gallop.
(Gallop around the room.)

Stop!
God is with us as we grow!
(Crouch down and slowly stand with arms above head.)

Shout a Verse

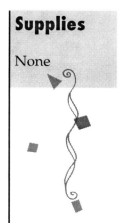

Have the children sit down on the floor or on chairs.

Say: Let's say the Bible verse together. I will say the first part of the verse. When you hear me say "up," jump up and shout the second part of the verse, "the LORD was with him."

Say the first part of the verse with the children. Have the children jump up and shout the second part of the verse. Repeat the verse several times.

(Normal voice): **As Samuel grew UP,**
(Shout): **the LORD was with him.**

Whisper a Prayer

Say: Hannah prayed to God to ask God for a baby. God answered her prayer. Hannah had a baby boy named Samuel. God was with Samuel as he grew, and God is with us as we grow. We can pray to God anytime. That means we can talk to God anytime.

Have the children stand in a circle, holding hands. Sing the song printed below to the tune of "God Is so Good." Sing the first verse in a loud voice, the second verse in a normal voice, and the third verse in a soft voice. Have the children walk in a circle as you sing all the verses.

Shout out a prayer.	**Whisper a prayer.**
Shout out a prayer.	**Whisper a prayer.**
Shout out a prayer.	**Whisper a prayer.**
God will hear our prayers.	**God will hear our prayers.**

Sing out a prayer.
Sing out a prayer.
Sing out a prayer.
God will hear our prayers.

Have the children stop walking, but continue holding hands.

Say: Let's whisper a prayer to God right now. *(Whisper.)* **Thank you, God, for** *(name each child).* **Amen.**

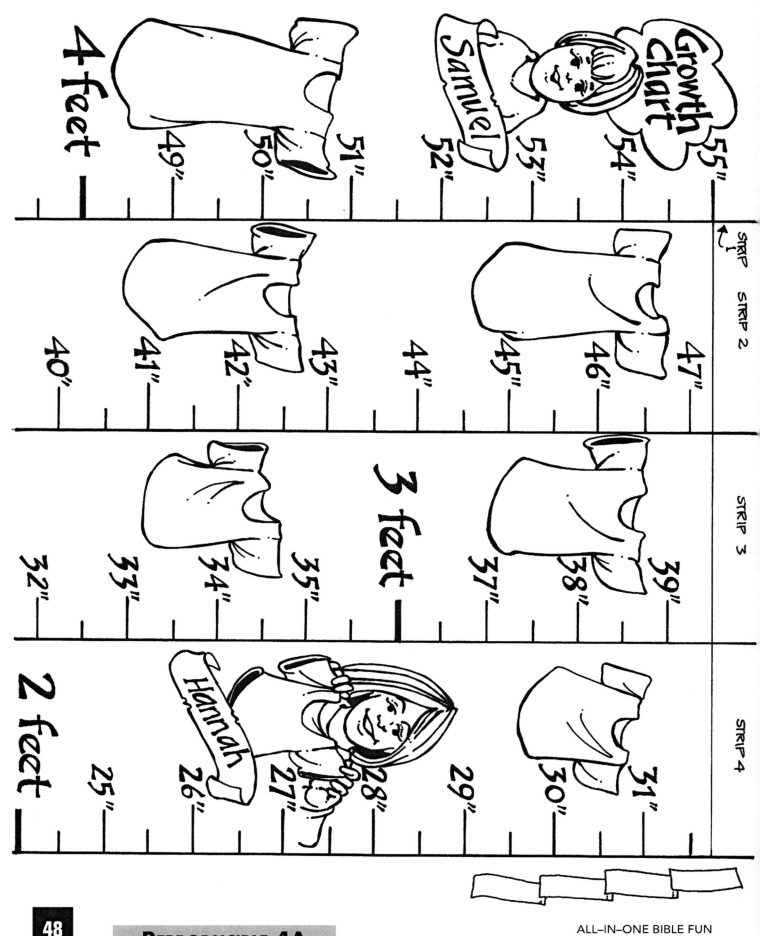

ALL-IN-ONE BIBLE FUN

Name

Look at me,
I'm _____ years old.
I'm _____ inches tall.
I'm growing!

**All-in-One
BIBLE** PRESCHOOL
FUN

Samuel Listens

Bible Verse

As Samuel grew up, the LORD was with him.

1 Samuel 3:19

Bible Story

1 Samuel 3:1-19

Hannah kept the promise she made to God. Surely she must have felt that Samuel had been chosen by God for some special purpose. In sharp contrast to Hannah's delight with her son was Eli's despair over his sons. Time and time again they showed complete disregard for God's laws. According to the customs of the day, the priesthood should have passed from Eli to his descendants, but because of the moral and cultic violations committed by Eli's sons, God withdrew God's blessing from the house of Eli.

Although Samuel stayed on as Eli's assistant in the temple at Shiloh, Hannah and Elkanah remained faithful to their son. Each year they visited him when they came to worship in the temple, and Hannah brought him a new cloak she had made. God continued to bless Hannah, and she bore five more sons.

Although still young, Samuel took an active role in service in the temple. His duties in the temple likely would have included fill-

ing and lighting the lamp, which played an important part in religious practices. Opening and closing the temple doors probably meant more than just the physical act; travelers likely were asking the young man for advice. Still, Samuel had not had a personal experience with God.

When God first spoke to Samuel, Samuel assumed it was Eli calling him. It took an older, experienced Eli to realize finally that the voice Samuel was hearing was God's.

After the visit from God the focus began to shift from Eli to Samuel. In time Samuel became a great leader, prophet, and priest. He was respected by the people and favored by God.

Help your children understand that God speaks to us in many ways. Be a model of God's love and acceptance for them.

God is with us as we grow.

If time is limited, we recommend those activities that are noted in **boldface**. Depending on your time and the number of children, you may be able to include more activities.

ACTIVITY	TIME	SUPPLIES	
Samuel Puppet Pop-ups	**15 minutes**	**Reproducible 5A, scissors, crayons, glue or tape, craft sticks**	JOIN THE FUN
Listen 'n Do	10 minutes	None	
Hannah's Hop	5 minutes	None	BIBLE STORY FUN
Bible Story: Samuel! Samuel!	**10 minutes**	**puppets from "Samuel Puppet Pop-ups" activity (Reproducible 5A)**	
Bible Verse Fun	**5 minutes**	**Bible**	
Listen Lessons	10 minutes	Reproducible 5B, scissors	
Sing!	5 minutes	None	
Pop a Verse	5 minutes	puppets from "Samuel Puppet Pop-ups" activity (Reproducible 5A)	LIVE THE FUN
Whisper a Prayer	**5 minutes**	**None**	

Supplies

Reproducible 5A, scissors, crayons, glue or tape, craft sticks

Samuel Puppet Pop-ups

Photocopy and cut out the Samuel puppet pop-up **(Reproducible 5A)** for each child. Let the children decorate the puppet pieces with crayons.

Say: Today our Bible story is about Samuel. Samuel grew from a baby to a boy. God was with Samuel as he grew.

> ## God is with us as we grow.

Show each child how to fold the mat with the puppet along the dotted lines. Glue or tape the sides of the mats together. Leave the top and bottom edges of the mats open. Help the children glue or tape the Samuel figure onto a craft stick. Show each child how to slide the Samuel puppet into the the pocket formed by the mat. Set the puppet pop-ups aside to use later in the lesson.

Supplies

None

Listen 'n Do

Have the children move to an open area of the room.

Say: Today our Bible story is about Samuel. Samuel grew from a baby to a boy. When Samuel was a boy, he helped Eli the priest in the temple. One night Samuel went to sleep on his mat. Then Samuel heard something that woke him up. Samuel had to listen very carefully to know what to do. Listen very carefully, and do what I tell you to do.

Call the children by name and give them two or three directions of things to do in sequence. Use the statements printed below as suggestions.

(Child's name), **touch your nose, touch your elbow, and touch your knee.**
(Child's name), **hop on one foot, touch the floor, and turn around.**
(Child's name), **jump once, clap your hands, and touch the floor.**
(Child's name), **wiggle your hips, stomp your foot, and bend your knees.**
(Child's name), **touch your toes, touch your ear, and rub your stomach.**
(Child's name), **touch your head, jump once, and wiggle your hips.**
(Child's name), **touch the floor, touch your nose, and touch your ears.**
(Child's name), **stomp one foot, touch your knee, and jump three times.**
(Child's name), **wiggle your hips, turn around, and touch the floor.**
(Child's name), **hop on one foot, touch the floor, and turn around.**

Hannah's Hop

Supplies

None

Say: Today our Bible story is about Samuel, Hannah's son. Hannah wanted a baby. She prayed to God, and God answered her prayer. Hannah had a baby boy named Samuel. Samuel grew and grew. God was with Samuel as he grew.

Lead the children in hopping around the room as you say the following action poem for your children. End the hopping in your story area.

Hannah went to the temple
To talk to God in prayer.

So let's hop, hop here,
(Hop twice on one foot.)
And hop, hop there,
(Hop twice on the other foot.)
And hop, hop everywhere.
(Hop twice on both feet.)

She asked God for a baby boy
'Cause she knew God answered prayer.

So let's hop, hop here,
(Hop twice on one foot.)
And hop, hop there,
(Hop twice on the other foot.)
And hop, hop everywhere.
(Hop twice on both feet.)

Soon she had baby Samuel.
He was the answer to her prayer.

So let's hop, hop here,
(Hop twice on one foot.)
And hop, hop there,
(Hop twice on the other foot.)
And hop, hop everywhere.
(Hop twice on both feet.)

God was with Samuel as he grew.
Hannah thanked God with a prayer.

So let's hop, hop here,
(Hop twice on one foot.)
And hop, hop there,
(Hop twice on the other foot.)
And hop, hop everywhere.
(Hop twice on both feet.)

Samuel! Samuel!

by Daphna Flegal

Have the children hold their Samuel puppet pop-ups (Reproducible 5A) as you tell the story. Each time you say, "Samuel! Samuel!" have the children push the Samuel puppets up out of the sleeping mats. Then when you say, "Go back to sleep" have the children pull the Samuel puppets back inside the mats.

Samuel shut the **doors** to the **temple**. He checked the oil in the **lamp**. It was still burning. He took off his **coat**. Then Samuel spread out his **sleeping mat**. It was time for bed. Samuel laid down and went to sleep.

"Samuel! Samuel!" A voice called to Samuel in the night. *(Pop up the puppets.)*

Samuel woke up. He thought that **Eli** the priest had called him. He got up from his **sleeping mat** and put on his **coat**. He walked past the **oil lamp** and past the **doors** of the **temple** to the room where **Eli** was sleeping.

"Here I am," said Samuel sleepily.

Eli woke up. "Why are you here?" he asked Samuel.

"You called me," answered Samuel.

"No, I didn't," said **Eli**. "Go back to sleep." *(Pull the puppets back inside mats.)*

Samuel went back past the **doors** of the **temple** and the **oil lamp** to his **sleeping mat**. He took off his **coat** and laid down. Soon he was asleep.

"Samuel! Samuel!" A voice called Samuel's name again. *(Pop up the puppets.)*

Samuel woke up. He put on his **coat**. He walked past the **oil lamp** and past the **doors** of the **temple** to **Eli's** room.

"Here I am," said Samuel. "I heard you call my name."

"No, Samuel," said **Eli**. "I didn't call you. Go back to sleep." *(Pull the puppets back inside mats.)*

Samuel walked back past the the **oil lamp** and past the **doors** of the **temple** to his **sleeping mat**. He took off his **coat** and laid down. He went back to sleep.

"Samuel! Samuel!" The voice woke Samuel up a third time. *(Pop up the puppets.)*

Samuel put on his **coat**. He walked past the **oil lamp** and past the **doors** of the **temple** to **Eli**.

"I am not calling you," said **Eli**. "You must be hearing the voice of God. Go back to sleep. *(Pull the puppets back inside mats.)* If the voice calls to you again, say 'Speak, Lord, I am listening.'"

Samuel walked back past the **oil lamp** and past the **doors** of the **temple** to his **sleeping mat**. He took off his **coat** and laid down. He was very quiet. He wanted to hear the voice of God.

"Samuel! Samuel!" The voice of God called Samuel again. *(Pop up the puppets.)*

This time Samuel knew what to do. "Speak, Lord," said Samuel. "I am listening."

Bible Verse Fun

Choose a child to hold the Bible open to 1 Samuel 3:19.

Say: Today our Bible story is about Samuel. Samuel grew from a baby to a boy. God was with Samuel as he grew.

> ## God is with us as we grow.

Say the Bible verse, "As Samuel grew up, the LORD was with him" (1 Samuel 3:19), for the children. Have the children say the Bible verse after you.

Help the children learn the Bible verse by singing. Sing the words printed below to the tune of "The Farmer in the Dell." Clap in rhythm to the tune on the fourth line.

As Samuel grew up,
As Samuel grew up,
the LORD was with him,
(clap, clap, clap.)
As Samuel grew up.

Play a game with the children to reinforce the Bible verse. Begin the game with the children standing.

Say: Samuel helped Eli in the temple. When Eli told Samuel to go back to bed and listen to God, Samuel obeyed Eli. Let's play a game called "Eli Says." I will tell you to do certain things, but you should only do those things if I first say, "Eli says."

Eli says, clap your hands. *(Pause to allow the children time to do the command.)*
Eli says, say the Bible verse. *(Say the verse with the children.)*
Eli says, sit down. *(Have the children sit down on the floor or rug.)*
Yawn as big as you can. *(Remind the children that they should not yawn because you did not say "Eli says" first. Do not declare any children "out." Keep everyone in the game.)*
Eli says, close your eyes. *(Have the children close their eyes.)*
Eli says, go to sleep. *(Have the children pretend to sleep.)*
Wake up! *(Remind the children that they should not wake up because you did not say "Eli says" first.)*
Eli says, open your eyes. *(Have the children open their eyes.)*
Eli says, say the Bible verse. *(Say the verse with the children.)*
Eli says, stand up. *(Have the children stand up.)*
Stretch out your arms. *(Remind the children that they should not stretch their arms because you did not say "Eli says" first.)*
Eli says, say the Bible verse. *(Say the verse with the children.)*

Supplies

Reproducible 5B, scissors

Listen Lessons

Photocopy and cut out the story pictures **(Reproducible 5B).** Give each child one picture. Talk to the children about the pictures and make sure they know what their picture represents *(sleeping mat, temple, doors, oil lamp, Eli, and coat).*

Say: When Samuel was a boy, he helped Eli the priest in the temple. One night Samuel went to sleep on his mat. Then Samuel heard a voice calling to him. Whose voice did Samuel hear? *(God's)* **Listen very carefully to the story again. Each time you hear me say the name of your picture, jump up and show your picture. Then sit back down.**

Tell the children the story "Samuel! Samuel!" once again. Pause after each of the words printed in bold. Have the child holding that picture jump up and show your picture. Then have the child sit back down.

After telling the story **say: Samuel grew from a baby to a boy. When Samuel was a boy, he heard God's voice speaking to him. God was with Samuel as he grew.**

> ## God is with us as we grow.

Supplies

None

Sing!

Sing the song "Do You Hear Me?" to the tune of "Are You Sleeping?" Have the children move as suggested.

Do You Hear Me?
(Tune: "Are You Sleeping?")

Do you hear me,
(Cup one hand around ear.)
Do you hear me,
(Cup other hand around other ear.)
Sam-u-el?
(Cup hands around mouth, turn to left.)
Sam-u-el?
(Cup hands around mouth, turn to right.)

Yes, Lord, I am listening.
(Nod head yes.)
Yes, Lord, I am listening.
(Nod head yes.)
Here I am.
(Point to self with one hand.)
Here I am.
(Point to self with other hand.)

© 1997 Abingdon Press.

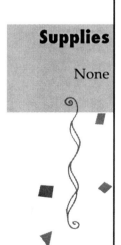

LIVE THE FUN

Pop a Verse

Say: Let's say the Bible verse together. I will say the first part of the verse. When you hear me say "up," push your Samuel puppet up out of the sleeping mat and say the second part of the verse, "the LORD was with him."

Say the first part of the verse with the children. Have the children push up their puppets and say the second part of the verse. Repeat the verse several times.

As Samuel grew UP, *(Push up the puppet.)*
the LORD was with him.

Whisper a Prayer

Say: Hannah prayed to God to ask God for a baby. God answered her prayer. Hannah had a baby boy named Samuel. God was with Samuel as he grew, and God is with us as we grow. We can pray to God anytime. That means we can talk to God anytime.

Have the children stand in a circle, holding hands. Sing the song printed below to the tune of "God Is So Good." Sing the first verse in a loud voice, the second verse in a normal voice, and the third verse in a soft voice. Have the children walk in a circle as you sing all the verses.

Shout out a prayer.
Shout out a prayer.
Shout out a prayer.
God will hear our prayers.

Whisper a prayer.
Whisper a prayer.
Whisper a prayer.
God will hear our prayers.

Sing out a prayer.
Sing out a prayer.
Sing out a prayer.
God will hear our prayers.

Have the children stop walking, but continue holding hands.

Say: Let's whisper a prayer to God right now. *(Whisper.)* Thank you, God, for *(name each child)*. Amen.

Supplies

puppets from "Samuel Puppet Pop-ups" activity (Reproducible 5B)

Supplies

None

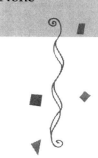

FOLD

FOLD

GLUE OR TAPE

GLUE

REPRODUCIBLE 5A

REPRODUCIBLE 5B

All-in-One
BIBLE PRESCHOOL
FUN

David and Samuel

Bible Verse

The LORD looks on the heart.

1 Samuel 16:7

Bible Story

1 Samuel 16:1-13

God sent Samuel to Bethlehem in search of a new king after God rejected Saul. Saul had proven himself as a military leader, but he had begun to make decisions on his own that went against the word of God. The sin for which Saul was rejected was that of self-will or disobedience. Samuel grieved for Saul, but he knew he must obey God and anoint a new king.

When Samuel arrived in Bethlehem, he explained to the people that he had come to make a sacrifice to the Lord. He consecrated Jesse and his sons and invited them to the sacrifice. One by one the handsome sons of Jesse passed in front of Samuel. Each time Samuel expected to hear the voice of the Lord telling him to anoint one of them king. But God was silent. Finally he asked Jesse if all his sons were present. There was just the youngest, Jesse replied, away tending the sheep. When David arrived, Samuel heard the voice of the Lord say, "Rise and anoint him; he is the one."

Point out to your children that even though all the sons of Jesse were handsome, God looked past outward appearances and saw in David, the youngest son, an inner quality necessary for a king. As a teacher you can affirm your children by looking past their outward appearances. Praise the children you teach for their actions and for their attitudes, not for how they look or what they are wearing. Say things such as, "Ruth, I like your happy smile today," or "Matt, I like the way you help clean up," instead of, "Ruth, what a pretty dress you are wearing today," or "Matt, what great hair you have."

It is never too early to introduce children to God's abiding love. Under your guidance the children you teach can begin to understand that God is with them for comfort and guidance. God is always with us. God always loves us.

We can show love to God and to others.

If time is limited, we recommend those activities that are noted in **boldface**. Depending on your time and the number of children, you may be able to include more activities.

ACTIVITY	TIME	SUPPLIES	
Crown o' Hearts	**10 minutes**	**Reproducible 6A; scissors; crayons; glue, tape, or stapler and staples; basket or bag**	JOIN THE FUN
Name That Heart	10 minutes	Reproducible 6B; dark permanent marker *(teacher use only);* yellow, blue, or light-pink highlighter markers; glue sticks; colored cellophane	
David's Dance	5 minutes	None	
Bible Story: A Loving Heart	**10 minutes**	**heart crowns from "Crown o'Hearts" activity (Reproducible 6A)**	BIBLE STORY FUN
Bible Verse Fun	**5 minutes**	**Bible; Reproducible 6B; masking tape; six beanbags, sponge balls, or balls of crumpled scrap paper; basket or bucket**	
Sign a Verse	5 minutes	None	
Sing!	5 minutes	None	
Hearts 'n Hands	5 minutes	None	LIVE THE FUN
Prayerful Hearts	**5 minutes**	**heart crowns from "Crown o'Hearts activity" (Reproducible 6A), basket or bag**	

Crown o' Hearts

Photocopy and cut out the heart crown **(Reproducible 6A)** for each child. Give each child a heart piece. Let the children color the heart pieces with crayons.

Say: Today our Bible story is about Samuel and David. Samuel grew into a man. When he was a man, God sent him to find a new king. God had Samuel choose a young boy named David to be the new king. God chose David because God knew David had a loving heart. That meant that David loved God and others.

> ## We can show love to God and to others.

Help each child glue, tape, or staple the ends of the crown pieces together to make one long strip. If you use staples, make sure the prongs of the staples are facing outward, away from the child's head. Write the child's name on the strip. Measure the crown strip around each child's head. Tape, glue, or staple the ends of the crown strip together. Have the children place their crowns in a large basket or bag.

Supplies

Reproducible 6B; dark permanent marker *(teacher use only)*; yellow, blue, or light-pink high-lighter markers; glue sticks; colored cellophane

Name That Heart

Photocopy the heart **(Reproducible 6B)** for each child.

Say: God had Samuel choose David to be king because God knew David had a loving heart. That meant that David loved God and others. These hearts can help us remember that we can be like David. We can love God and others.

Give each child a heart picture. Use a dark permanent marker to write the child's name in the center of the heart.

Say: (Child's name), you have a loving heart. You can love God and others.

Encourage the children to decorate the hearts with yellow, blue, or light-pink highlighter markers. Show the children how their names will show through the highlighter markers.

Or give the children glue sticks and small pieces of colored cellophane. Let the children glue the colored cellophane to their hearts. The children's names will show through the cellophane.

David's Dance

Supplies

None

Say: Today our Bible story is about Samuel and David. Samuel grew into a man. When he was a man, God sent him to find a new king. God had Samuel choose a young boy named David to be the new king. God chose David because God knew David had a loving heart. David loved God and others.

 We can show love to God and to others.

Lead the children in moving around the room as you say the following action poem for your children. End the movement in your story area.

Step, step, step around the room.
(Walk around the room.)
Now let's stop and sing.
(Stop, put hands around mouth.)
David had a loving heart.
(Cross hands over heart.)
God chose him to be king.
(Pretend to put crown on head.)

March, march, march around the room.
(March around the room.)
Now let's stop and sing.
(Stop, put hands around mouth.)
David had a loving heart.
(Cross hands over heart.)
God chose him to be king.
(Pretend to put crown on head.)

Hop, hop, hop around the room.
(Hop around the room.)
Now let's stop and sing.
(Stop, put hands around mouth.)
David had a loving heart.
(Cross hands over heart.)
God chose him to be king.
(Pretend to put crown on head.)

A Loving Heart

by Daphna Flegal

*Encourage the children to wear their heart crowns (**Reproducible 6A**) and to sit down in your story area.*

Say: Our Bible story is about Samuel and David. When Samuel was a man, God sent him to find a new king. God had Samuel choose a young boy named David to be the new king. God chose David because God knew David had a loving heart. Each time you hear me say, "The LORD looks on the heart," stand up and repeat the words after me.

Samuel loved God with all his heart.

The LORD looks on the heart. *(Have the children stand and repeat the verse.)*

One day God wanted Samuel to find a new king. God wanted the king to be someone who had a loving heart.

The LORD looks on the heart. *(Have the children stand and repeat the verse.)*

God sent Samuel to Bethlehem to see a man named Jesse. "One of Jesse's sons will be the new king," God said to Samuel. "One of his sons has a loving heart."

The LORD looks on the heart. *(Have the children stand and repeat the verse.)*

Samuel went to Bethlehem. He met Jesse's oldest son. He was very handsome, but God did not choose him to be the new king.

The LORD looks on the heart. *(Have the children stand and repeat the verse.)*

Samuel met Jesse's second son, but God did not choose him to be the new king.

The LORD looks on the heart. *(Have the children stand and repeat the verse.)*

Samuel met Jesse's third son, but God did not choose him to be the new king.

The LORD looks on the heart. *(Have the children stand and repeat the verse.)*

Jesse brought seven of his sons to meet Samuel. But God did not choose any of the seven sons to be the new king.

The LORD looks on the heart. *(Have the children stand and repeat the verse.)*

"Do you have any other sons?" Samuel asked Jesse.

"Yes," answered Jesse. "My youngest son is taking care of the sheep. His name is David."

Samuel met David, Jesse's youngest son. God did choose David to be the new king. David had a loving heart.

The LORD looks on the heart. *(Have the children stand and repeat the verse.)*

David had to wait until he grew to be a man to be king. God was with David as he grew. God knew David had a loving heart.

The LORD looks on the heart. *(Have the children stand and repeat the verse.)*

Bible Verse Fun

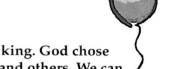

Choose a child to hold the Bible open to 1 Samuel 16:7.

Say: God had Samuel choose a young boy named David to be the new king. God chose David because God knew David had a loving heart. David loved God and others. We can have loving hearts.

We can show love to God and to others.

Say the Bible verse, "The LORD looks on the heart." (1 Samuel 16:7), for the children. Have the children say the Bible verse after you.

Help the children learn the Bible verse by singing. Sing the words printed below to the tune of "The Farmer in the Dell."

> "The LORD looks on the heart.
> The LORD looks on the heart."
> It doesn't matter who you are,
> "The LORD looks on the heart."

Play a game with the children to reinforce the Bible verse.

Photocopy the heart circle **(Reproducible 6B)**. Tape the heart to the floor. Tape a line of masking tape on the floor in front of the heart.

Provide six beanbags or sponge balls. Or make six paper balls by crumpling scrap paper into loose balls. Place the six beanbags or balls into a bucket or basket.

Choose a child to begin. Have the child stand behind the taped line. Give the child a bucket or basket with the balls.

Say: God chose David to be the new king because God knew David had a loving heart. Having a loving heart means that David loved God and loved others. We can show love to God and to others.

Have the child say the first word of the Bible verse and toss a ball onto the heart. Have the child say the second word of the Bible verse and toss a second ball. Continue until the child has completed the Bible verse and tossed all the balls. Give every child a turn.

Supplies

None

Sign a Verse

Teach the children the Bible verse, "The LORD looks on the heart" (1 Samuel 16:7), using signs from American Sign Language.

Lord — Make an "L" with the right hand. Place the "L" at the left shoulder and then move across the body to the right waist.

Look — Make a "Y" with one hand. Place the "Y" in front of the face with the palm facing the face. Turn the "Y" out so that the palm faces away from the face.

Heart — Draw an outline of a heart on the chest using an index finger.

Supplies

None

Sing!

Have the children move to an open area of the room. Sing the song "Loving Hearts" to the tune of "London Bridge" and play a game.

Choose a second teacher or a child to help you build a bridge with your arms (*like you were playing the game "London Bridge."*) Have the children line up to go under the bridge. Sing the song as the children march under the bridge. When you get to the end of the first verse, bring your arms down and capture the child walking under the bridge. Sing the second verse and use the captured child's name. Continue the singing game until all the children have been captured.

Loving Hearts
(*Tune: "London Bridge"*)

God saw David's loving heart,
loving heart, loving heart.
God saw David's loving heart
and chose him to be king.

(*Child's name*) has a loving heart,
loving heart, loving heart.
(*Child's name*) has a loving heart,
and shows (*his or her*) love to God.

Hearts 'n Hands

Have the children sit down on one side of the room.

Say: Having a loving heart means that we show love to God and to others. If I say something that shows love, clap your hands. If I say something that doesn't show love, keep your hands still.

We show love when we pray for one another. *(Clap hands.)*
We show love when we push and shove in line.
We show love when we share toys with our friends. *(Clap hands.)*
We show love when we sing praise to God. *(Clap hands.)*
We show love when we grab a toy away from a friend.
We show love when we say a Bible verse together. *(Clap hands.)*

Supplies

None

Prayerful Hearts

Have the children move to one side of the room. Collect the heart crowns **(Reproducible 6A)** and put them in a basket. Move to the opposite side of the room. Pick up one of the crowns from the basket or bag. Notice the child's name.

Say: I am looking for someone with a happy smile and a loving heart. I choose *(child's name)*. *(Child's name)*, hop to me.

Have the child hop to across the room you. Place the crown on the child's head.

Say: *(Child's name)* has a loving heart. *(Child's name)* loves God and others.

Continue until every child has moved across the room and received his or her crown. Vary how you tell each child to move *(march, gallop, crawl, jump, walk on tiptoe, walk with giant steps, walk with baby steps).*

Have each child sit down.

Say: It doesn't matter who we are or what we look like, God loves us. God loves *(name each child).*

Pray: Thank you, God, for *(name each child)*. Help *(name each child)* have loving hearts. Amen.

Supplies

heart crowns (Reproducible 6A), basket or bag

ALL–IN–ONE BIBLE FUN

REPRODUCIBLE 6B

All-in-One
BIBLE PRESCHOOL
FUN

David Plays the Harp

Bible Verse

The LORD looks on the heart.

1 Samuel 16:7

Bible Story

1 Samuel 16:14-23

Once Saul fell out of favor with God, he was at the mercy of his own ungovernable temperament. The Scriptures speak of an "evil spirit" or "evil force;" we see it as a depression. When he was in a deeply depressed state, he was not able to rule the kingdom.

His servants, searching for a way to comfort him, suggested the therapeutic value of music, and someone mentioned David to Saul. Saul sent for David, who arrived bearing gifts from his father, Jesse, and the first meeting between the current king and the man that God had chosen to replace him took place. David's musical therapy was successful and Saul took an instant liking to David, even making him his personal military aide. Probably at this point neither of them had any idea what was in store. As Saul's downward spiral was beginning, so was David's upward journey. Remember that, although God had rejected Saul as king because of Saul's rebellion, God still sent the remedy for Saul's melancholia through music.

David played a lyre, or harp, for Saul, a four-stringed instrument shaped like a flat box, with two arms joined by a crosspiece. David had spent many nights alone in the hills caring for his father's sheep. When the sheep were settled for the night, David sat on the hillside, playing his harp and singing his praises to God.

Young children respond to music. Music can set the tone for the moment or can provide a transition to the next activity. Quiet music can calm children; lively music can get them moving.

Sometimes your children will arrive upset or in a bad mood. Think of ways that you can comfort them. Perhaps one corner of the classroom can be turned into a quiet place for resting. Play quiet music and allow any child who wishes to curl up with blankets and pillows.

Preschoolers love being helpers. They can respond to the idea of helping others feel good. Give the children in your classroom opportunities to help others feel better.

We can help others feel better.

If time is limited, we recommend those activities that are noted in **boldface**. Depending on your time and the number of children, you may be able to include more activities.

ACTIVITY	TIME	SUPPLIES	
Musical Matchup	5 minutes	Reproducible 7A, scissors	JOIN THE FUN
Music Makers	**10 minutes**	**Reproducible 7A, scissors, basket or bag**	
David's Dance	5 minutes	None	BIBLE STORY FUN
Bible Story: David's Music	**10 minutes**	**None**	
Bible Verse Fun	**5 minutes**	**Bible, three different rhythm instruments or Reproducible 7A and scissors**	
Sign a Verse	5 minutes	None	
Sing!	5 minutes	None	
Dot-to-Dot Greetings	10 minutes	Reproducible 7B, nonpermanent markers, optional: music CD and CD player	LIVE THE FUN
Prayerful Hearts	**5 minutes**	**None**	

Musical Matchup

Photocopy at least two sets of the musical instrument pictures **(Reproducible 7A)**. Cut the pictures apart. Let the children match the pictures. Talk to the children about the instruments. Encourage the children to make the sounds of the instruments.

Say: Today our Bible story is about David. David played the harp and sang songs of praise to God. Sometimes David played the harp and sang songs to make others feel better.

> **We can help others feel better.**

Music Makers

Copy several sets of the musical instrument pictures **(Reproducible 7A)**, cut them out, and place in a basket or bag. Have the children sit in a circle. Give the basket or bag to one of the children in the circle.

Sing the first stanza of the song printed below to the tune of "Are You Sleeping?" Have the child holding the basket or bag pick out a picture. Sing the second stanza of the song using the name of whatever instrument is illustrated on the picture. After the song have everyone pretend to play the instrument that was named. Repeat until everyone has picked a musical instrument picture.

> Music maker, music maker,
> What can you play?
> What can you play?
>
> I can play the *(name instrument)*.
> I can play the *(name instrument)*.
> Listen as I play.
> Listen as I play.

Instruments and their sounds include:
Harp—*pluck, pluck, pluck*
Guitar—*strum, strum, strum*
Trumpet—*toot, toot, toot*
Drum—*boom, boom, boot*
Flute—*tweet, tweet, tweet.*
Tuba—*oompah, oompah, oompah*

David's Dance

Say: Today our Bible story is about David. David played the harp and sang songs of praise to God. Sometimes David played the harp and sang songs to make others feel better. King Saul was very unhappy. David played his harp for King Saul. David's music made King Saul feel better.

Supplies

None

 We can help others feel better.

Lead the children in moving around the room as you say the following action poem for your children. End the movement in your story area.

Step, step, step around the room.
(Walk around the room.)
Now let's stop and sing.
(Stop, put hands around mouth.)
David played the harp for Saul,
(Pretend to play a harp.)
A most unhappy king.
(Pretend to put crown on head.)

March, march, march around the room.
(March around the room.)
Now let's stop and sing.
(Stop, put hands around mouth.)
David played the harp for Saul,
(Pretend to play a harp.)
A most unhappy king.
(Pretend to put crown on head.)

Hop, hop, hop around the room.
(Hop around the room.)
Now let's stop and sing.
(Stop, put hands around mouth.)
David played the harp for Saul,
(Pretend to play a harp.)
A most unhappy king.
(Pretend to put crown on head.)

David's Music

by Daphna Flegal

Have the children stand in a circle. Tell the story and do the suggested motions. Encourage the children to do the motions with you.

"Ohhh, ohhh, ohhh!" cried King Saul. *(Hold head in hands, lean head to one side.)* He slumped down on the throne.

"Ohhh, ohhh, ohhh!" *(Hold head in hands, lean head to other side.)* King Saul put his head in his hands.

"Ohhh, ohhh, ohhh!" cried King Saul. *(Hold head in hands, lean head to other side.)* "I am so unhappy!"

"I have an idea," said one of King Saul's servants. *(Point index finger to side of head.)* "Maybe David could play his harp for you. Maybe his music would help you feel better."

"Ohhh, ohhh, ohhh!" cried King Saul. *(Hold head in hands, lean head to one side.)* "Send David to me."

The servants brought David to King Saul. *(Walk in place.)*

"Ohhh, ohhh, ohhh!" cried King Saul. *(Hold head in hands, lean head to other side.)* "I hope your music will make me feel better."

David began to play his harp for unhappy King Saul. *(Pretend to play a harp.)*

Pluck, pluck, pluck. David's music filled the room. *(Pretend to play a harp.)*

Pluck, pluck, pluck. David's music was gentle and calm. *(Pretend to play a harp.)*

Pluck, pluck, pluck. David's music was sweet and clear. *(Pretend to play a harp.)*

"Ahhh, ahhh, ahhh," sighed King Saul. *(Sigh.)* "David's music makes me feel calm."

"Ahhh, ahhh, ahhh," sighed King Saul. *(Sigh.)* "David's music makes me feel happy."

"Ahhh, ahhh, ahhh," sighed King Saul. *(Sigh.)* "David's music makes me feel better."

Bible Verse Fun

Choose a child to hold the Bible open to 1 Samuel 16:7.

Say: Today our Bible story is about David. David played the harp and sang songs of praise to God. Sometimes David played the harp and sang songs to make others feel better. King Saul was very unhappy. David played his harp for King Saul. David's music made King Saul feel better. David showed love to King Saul. David had a loving heart.

We can help others feel better.

Say the Bible verse, "The LORD looks on the heart" (1 Samuel 16:7), for the children. Have the children say the Bible verse after you.

Help the children learn the Bible verse by singing. Sing the words printed below to the tune of "The Farmer in the Dell."

> "The LORD looks on the heart.
> The LORD looks on the heart."
> It doesn't matter who you are,
> "The LORD looks on the heart."

Play a game with the children to reinforce the Bible verse.

Have the children move to one side of the room and stand in a single line. Place three rhythm instruments on the opposite side of the room. You might use a drum, a rattle, rhythm sticks, a bell, or wood blocks for the rhythm instruments.

Say: David had a loving heart. He showed love to King Saul when he played his harp and helped King Saul feel better. When we help others feel better, we are showing love.

Have each child run to the musical instruments, pick up and play each one, run back to the next child in line, and then say the Bible verse, "The LORD looks on the heart" (1 Samuel 16:7). Continue the relay until every child has a turn.

If rhythm instruments are not available, photocopy and cut apart the instrument pictures **(Reproducible 7A)**. Use the pictures instead of the rhythm instruments. Have the children run to the pictures, pick them up, and make the sounds the instruments would make.

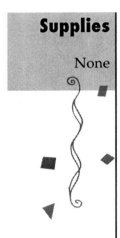

Supplies

None

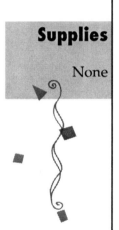

Supplies

None

Sign a Verse

Teach the children the Bible verse, "The LORD looks on the heart" (1 Samuel 16:7), using signs from American Sign Language.

Lord — Make an "L" with the right hand. Place the "L" at the left shoulder and then move across the body to the right waist.

Look — Make a "Y" with one hand. Place the "Y" in front of the face with the palm facing the face. Turn the "Y" out so that the palm faces away from the face.

Heart — Draw an outline of a heart on the chest using an index finger.

Sing!

Have the children move to an open area of the room. Sing the song "David Played the Harp" to the tune of "The Farmer in the Dell." Encourage the children to pretend to strum a harp as you sing the song together.

David Played the Harp
(Tune: "The Farmer in the Dell")

Young David played the harp,
Young David played the harp,
He sang songs of praise to God.
Young David played the harp,
(Pretend to strum a harp.)

Young David played the harp,
Young David played the harp,
King Saul felt better when he heard
Young David played the harp,
(Pretend to strum a harp.)

Lord

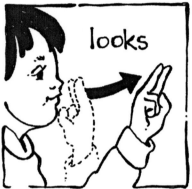

looks

heart

Dot-to-Dot Greetings

Supplies

Reproducible 7B, nonpermanent markers, optional: music CD and CD player

Photocopy the get-well cards **(Reproducible 7B)** for each child. Read the message on the card to the children.

Say: David helped King Saul feel better. We can help other people feel better. Let's decorate these get-well cards. We will give them to people in our church who are sick. Your cards will help them feel better.

Have the children turn the cards to the blank side. Have each child choose a marker. Sing "David Played the Harp" (page 76). Encourage the children to make dots with a marker while you sing. Stop singing. Have each child choose a different marker. Sing again. Have the children use the second marker and draw lines to connect the dots anyway they wish. If you do not wish to sing, use a music CD. Start and stop the music for the activity.

Remind the children that their cards will help people who are sick feel better.

Prayerful Hearts

Supplies

None

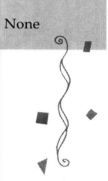

Have the children move to one side of the room. Move to the opposite side of the room.

Say: I am looking for someone with a happy smile and a loving heart. I choose (child's name). (Child's name), hop to me.

Have the child hop to across the room you. Have the child hold out his or her hand. Use your index finger to lightly draw a heart shape on the child's palm.

Say: (Child's name) has a loving heart. (Child's name) loves God and others.

Continue until every child has moved across the room and received his or her blessing. Vary how you tell each child to move (march, gallop, crawl, jump, walk on tiptoe, walk with giant steps, walk with baby steps).

Have each child sit down.

Say: It doesn't matter who we are or what we look like, God loves us. God loves (name each child).

Pray: Thank you, God, for (name each child). Help (name each child) have loving hearts. Amen.

REPRODUCIBLE 7A

REPRODUCIBLE 7B

79

All-in-One
BIBLE PRESCHOOL
FUN

David and Jonathan

Bible Verse

A friend loves at all times.

Proverbs 17:17

Bible Story

1 Samuel 18:1–4

The friendship that developed between David and Jonathan is one of the strongest bonds recorded in the Old Testament. These two men vowed that their friendship and loyalty to each other would be broken only by death; even then, they promised, their loyalty to each other would be extended to the family of the deceased. Years later, David brought to his court the only living son of Jonathan and restored to him all the land that had belonged to his grandfather, Saul.

It is especially important to note that Jonathan gave David his robe, armor, sword, bow, and belt. As King Saul's son, Jonathan would have been in line to be king after Saul's death. When he gave his clothes and armor to David, he was symbolically passing his birthright on to David, the one God had chosen to be king. When David accepted the gifts and wore them, he was assuming the role of crown prince, heir to the throne.

But while David's friendship with Jonathan grew stronger, David's relationship with Saul deteriorated. Saul became a man out of control. He was consumed by jealousy and was determined to kill David. Even though it meant defying his father, Jonathan helped David escape Saul's rage.

Friendships are important to everyone, even children. Three- and four-year-olds enjoy having friends and will often consider whoever is playing with them at that moment their friend. They need opportunities to learn to coexist with others in settings where there are loving adults to guide their activities. You can help by teaching and modeling positive ways of playing together. You can set limits, offer opportunities for sharing to take place, and praise your children for working together.

Friends show love to one another.

If time is limited, we recommend those activities that are noted in **boldface**. Depending on your time and the number of children, you may be able to include more activities.

ACTIVITY	TIME	SUPPLIES	
Find a Friend	**5 minutes**	**Reproducible 8A, scissors, tape**	JOIN THE FUN
Friendship Feats	10 minutes	None	
David's Dance	5 minutes	None	BIBLE STORY FUN
Bible Story: Very Good Friends	**10 minutes**	**None**	
Bible Verse Fun	**5 minutes**	**Bible; Reproducibles 8A, 8B, and 6A; scissors; masking tape**	
Sign a Verse	5 minutes	None	
Sing!	5 minutes	None	
Friendship Follies	10 minutes	None	LIVE THE FUN
Prayerful Hearts	**5 minutes**	**None**	

Supplies

Reproducible 8A, scissors, tape

Find a Friend

Photocopy and cut out the friendship bracelets **(Reproducible 8A)**.

Save the David's belt picture to use later in the lesson. Make enough copies so that two children will have the same kind of bracelet. If you have an uneven number of children, you will need to wear one of the bracelets.

Say: Today our Bible story is about David and Jonathan. David and Jonathan were very good friends. They showed love to each other.

> ### Friends show love to one another.

Let each child choose a friendship bracelet. Have the child identify the picture on the bracelet. Tape the bracelet around the child's wrist.

Have the children move to an open area of the room. Clap your hands repeatedly. Have the children move around the room as you clap your hands. Stop clapping. Have the children find the friend who is wearing the same kind of bracelet. Clap again and have the pairs of friends dance together while you are clapping.

Supplies

None

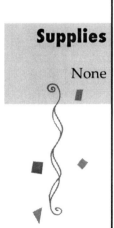

Friendship Feats

Have each pair of friends stand on one side of the room. Make sure there is space to move between each pair. Have each pair of children move together across the room as directed. Clap for all the children as they finish.

Friends, put your hands on your shoulders, now walk across the room.
Friends, put your hands on your hips, now hop across the room.
Friends, put your hands above your head, now tiptoe across the room.
Friends, put your hands at your sides, now hop on one foot across the room.
Friends, put your hands on your head, now walk backwards across the room.
Friends, put your hands on your knees, now take baby steps across the room.
Friends, hold the hand of your friend, now gallop together across the room.

David's Dance

Say: Today our Bible story is about David and Jonathan. Jonathan was the son of King Saul. David and Jonathan were very good friends. They promised that they would always be friends.

 Friends show love to one another.

Lead the children in moving around the room as you say the following action poem. End the movement in your story area.

Step, step, step around the room.
(Walk around the room.)
Now let's stop and sing.
(Stop, put hands around mouth.)
David had a friend he loved.
(Cross hands over heart.)
The son of Saul, the king.
(Pretend to put crown on head.)

March, march, march around the room.
(March around the room.)
Now let's stop and sing.
(Stop, put hands around mouth.)
David had a friend he loved.
(Cross hands over heart.)
The son of Saul, the king.
(Pretend to put crown on head.)

Hop, hop, hop around the room.
(Hop around the room.)
Now let's stop and sing.
(Stop, put hands around mouth.)
David had a friend he loved.
(Cross hands over heart.)
The son of Saul, the king.
(Pretend to put crown on head.)

Very Good Friends

by Daphna Flegal

Have the children stand in a circle. Tell the children the story. Have the children repeat the refrain and do the motions each time the refrain appears in the story.

David lived with King Saul. He became friends with King Saul's son, Jonathan.

**David and Jonathan
were very good friends.
Stomp, stomp, clap, clap,**
(Stomp twice; clap twice.)
Stretch and bend.
(Stretch arms over head; bend over.)

One day Jonathan wanted to give David a special gift. He gave David his robe and his belt.

**David and Jonathan
were very good friends.
Stomp, stomp, clap, clap,**
(Stomp twice; clap twice.)
Stretch and bend.
(Stretch arms over head; bend over.)

David knew that the robe and belt were special to Jonathan. He was happy to have Jonathan's gift. David put on the robe and belt.

**David and Jonathan
were very good friends.
Stomp, stomp, clap, clap,**
(Stomp twice; clap twice.)
Stretch and bend.
(Stretch arms over head; bend over.)

David and Jonathan made a promise to each other. They promised that they would always be very good friends.

**David and Jonathan
were very good friends.
Stomp, stomp, clap, clap,**
(Stomp twice; clap twice.)
Stretch and bend.
(Stretch arms over head; bend over.)

David and Jonathan kept their promise to each other. They helped each other. They showed love to each other.

**David and Jonathan
were very good friends.
Stomp, stomp, clap, clap,**
(Stomp twice; clap twice.)
Stretch and bend.
(Stretch arms over head; bend over.)

Bible Verse Fun

Choose a child to hold the Bible open to Proverbs 17:17.

Say: Today our Bible story is about David and Jonathan. David and Jonathan were very good friends. They showed love to each other.

Friends show love to one another.

Say the Bible verse, "A friend loves at all times" (Proverbs 17:17), for the children. Have the children say the Bible verse after you.

Help the children learn the Bible verse by singing. Sing the words printed below to the tune of "She'll Be Coming 'Round the Mountain."

> "Oh, the Bible says a friend loves at all times.
> "Oh, the Bible says a friend loves at all times.
>   Just like Jonathan and David,
>   Just like Jonathan and David.
> "Oh, the Bible says a friend loves at all times.
>
> © 1999 Abingdon Press

Play a game with the children to reinforce the Bible verse. Photocopy the David picture **(Reproducible 8B)**. Tape the picture on a door or wall where the children can easily reach it. Photocopy and cut out the belt picture on the friendship bracelet page **(Reproducible 8A)** so that you have a belt for each child. Give each child a belt.

Say: Jonathan gave his friend David his robe and his belt. In our picture David does not have the belt. Let's give David Jonathan's belt.

Play the game like "Pin the Tail on the Donkey." Have the children come one at a time to stand in front of David's picture. Put a loop of masking tape on the back of the belts. Use the heart crown **(Reproducible 6A)** to make a paper blindfold. Let each child try to place the belt on David's picture.

After each child places the belt on the picture, repeat the Bible verse with the children, "A friend loves at all times" (Proverbs 17:17).

Supplies

None

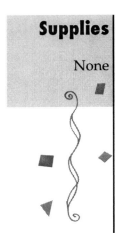

Sign a Verse

Teach the children the Bible verse, "A friend loves at all times" (Proverbs 17:17), using signs from American Sign Language.

Friend — Hook the right index finger over the left index finger. Reverse.

Loves — Cross hands at wrists and press over your heart.

All — Hold the left hand with palm towards the body. Circle right hand out and around the left palm. End with the back of the right hand in the left palm.

Times — Tap the back of the left hand with the right index finger.

Supplies

None

Sing!

Have the children move to an open area of the room. Sing the song "David and Jonathan" to the tune of "Are You Sleeping?" Encourage the children to do the suggested motions as you sing the song together.

David and Jonathan
(Tune: "Are You Sleeping?")

Here is David, here is Jonathan.
*(Hold up index finger on one hand;
hold up index finger on other hand.)*
They are friends, they are friends.
*(Make the sign for friend: Hook the right index finger
over the left index finger. Reverse.)*
They both made a promise,
(Put hands over heart.)
they'd be friends forever.
(Clasp hands together.)
They are friends, they are friends.
*(Make the sign for friend: Hook the right index finger
over the left index finger. Reverse.)*

Words: Sharilyn S. Adair and Daphna Flegal © 1997 Abingdon Press

friend

loves

all

times

Friendship Follies

Supplies

None

If you did the "Find a Friend" activity, have the children find their bracelet **(Reproducible 8A)** partners and stand together in an open area of the room. Say the following statements and chant for the children. Have the children clap their hands and move as suggested.

A friend loves when you're sad.
A friend, a friend,
(Clap hands on the word "friend.")
A friend loves at all times,
(Clap hands on "friend" and "all.")
So let's get nose to nose.
(Touch noses with partner.)

A friend loves when you're here.
A friend, a friend,
(Clap hands on the word "friend.")
A friend loves at all times,
(Clap hands on "friend" and "all.")
So let's get hip to hip.
(Touch hips with partners.)

A friend loves when you're happy.
A friend, a friend,
(Clap hands on the word "friend.")
A friend loves at all times,
(Clap hands on "friend" and "all.")
So let's get elbow to elbow.
(Touch elbows with partners.)

A friend loves when you're away.
A friend, a friend,
(Clap hands on the word "friend.")
A friend loves at all times,
(Clap hands on "friend" and "all.")
So let's get knee to knee.
(Touch knees with partners.)

Prayerful Hearts

Supplies

None

Have the children move to one side of the room. Move to the opposite side of the room.

Say: I am looking for a loving friend. I choose *(child's name).*
(Child's name), **hop to me.**

Have the child hop to across the room you. Have the child hold out his or her hand. Use your index finger to lightly draw a heart shape on the child's palm.

Say: *(Child's name)* **is a loving friend. Friends show love to one another.**

Continue until every child has moved across the room and received his or her blessing. Vary how you tell each child to move *(march, gallop, crawl, jump, walk on tiptoe, walk with giant steps, walk with baby steps).*

Have each child sit down.

Pray: Thank you, God, for *(name each child).* **Help** *(name each child)* **be a loving friend. Amen.**

ALL–IN–ONE BIBLE FUN

REPRODUCIBLE 8B

89

All-in-One BIBLE FUN PRESCHOOL

The Two Houses

Bible Verse

God is love.

1 John 4:8

Bible Story

Matthew 7:24-27

From his work with Joseph, Jesus would have learned many things about carpentry and building. Perhaps that is why he used the image of building a house in this parable.

During Jesus' time in Palestine there were many dry creek beds called "wadi." Today modern drainage systems handle much of the seasonal run-off, but that was not true in biblical times. Such a stream bed was sandy, and a foolish builder, or someone unfamiliar with the land, might choose to build there because the soil could be dug more easily than farther up the slope. A house could be easily constructed from stones found right at hand. All would be well until the rains came, when the dry bed would become a raging torrent.

In this parable Jesus is cautioning us to take care how we build our lives. Showing the love of God to others is one sure way to prepare a firm foundation. Words are not enough; we must put love into action.

Help your children think of ways of putting our love for God into action to help other people. Sharing is a critical part of a young child's social development. Always look for ways a child can share toys or materials in the classroom, and remind children that sharing shows love.

Children also can express love for others they know by making and sharing gifts, doing chores, or sending illustrated greetings to friends. Children can learn that God calls us to show our love for neighbors we do not know by becoming involved in churchwide projects of caring such as food banks, clothing collections, or soup kitchens. Remind your children that God loves everyone, and as followers of God, we are to do the same.

We can learn about God's love.

If time is limited, we recommend those activities that are noted in **boldface**. Depending on your time and the number of children, you may be able to include more activities.

ACTIVITY	TIME	SUPPLIES	
Storybook Sashay	**15 minutes**	**Reproducibles 9A and 9B, scissors, 4 sets of crayons, stapler and staples**	JOIN THE FUN
Sandbox Stories	10 minutes	sponge, plastic tub or metal cake pan, sand, flat rock, pitcher, water	
Parable Parade	5 minutes	None	BIBLE STORY FUN
Sign 'n Say	5 minutes	None	
Bible Story: The Two Houses	**10 minutes**	**storybooks from "Storybook Sashay" activity (Reproducibles 9A and 9B)**	
Bible Verse Fun	**10 minutes**	**Bible, scrap paper**	
Sing!	5 minutes	None	
House Painting	10 minutes	storybooks from "Storybook Sashay" activity (Reproducibles 9A and 9B), newspaper, smocks, sponge paintbrushes, tempera paint, shallow tray, construction paper, scissors, stapler and staples	
Love Lessons	5 minutes	None	LIVE THE FUN
Parable Prayers	**5 minutes**	**construction paper, scissors**	

Supplies

Reproducibles 9A and 9B, scissors, 4 sets of crayons, stapler and staples

Storybook Sashay

Photocopy and cut apart the storybook pages **(Reproducibles 9A and 9B)** for each child. Place all the first pages of the storybook and a set of crayons on one table or on the floor in one area of the room. Place all the second pages and a set of crayons on another table or on the floor in another area of the room. Place all the third pages and a set of crayons in a third area of the room. Place all the fourth pages and a set of crayons in a fourth area of the room.

Say: **Today our Bible story is a story Jesus told about two houses. Jesus told this story to help people learn about God's love.**

We can learn about God's love.

Have the children start at the first area. Let the children use crayons to decorate the first page of the storybooks. Then have the children bring their first pages and move to the second area to decorate the second page of their storybooks. Have the children continue to move around the room until they have completed all four pages of their storybooks. Help each child stack the pages in the correct order from 1 to 4. Staple the pages together along the left-hand side. Save the storybooks to use later in the lesson.

Sandbox Stories

Supplies

sponge, plastic tub or metal cake pan, sand, flat rock, pitcher, water

Say: **Jesus told a story about two houses. One house was built on the sand.**

Place a plastic tub or a metal cake pan on the table. Place sand in the bottom of the tub or pan. Let the children enjoy playing in the small sandbox. Show the children the sponge. Tell the children to pretend that the sponge is a house.

Place the sponge on a pile of sand. Pour water in the bottom of the tub or pan to wash away the pile of sand and to make the sponge fall.

Say: **When it rained, the house built on the sand fell down.**

Place a flat rock in the bottom of the tub or pan. Place the sponge on the rock. Pour water in the bottom of the tub or pan. Show the children that the sponge stays on the rock.

Say: **When it rained, the house on the rock did not fall down. Jesus told this story to help people learn about God's love.**

Parable Parade

Say: The stories Jesus told are called parables. Let's say the word *parable*. (*Have the children repeat it.*) **Let's have a parable parade.**

Use the following movement poem to lead your children to the story area.

Supplies

None

Let's have a parable parade	**Let's have a story stomp**
(*March around the room.*)	(*Stomp around the room.*)
And wave our arms up high.	**And wave our arms down low.**
(*Wave arms above head.*)	(*Wave arms down low.*)
Let's have a parable parade	**Let's have a story stomp**
(*March around the room.*)	(*Stomp around the room.*)
And try to reach the sky.	**And wiggle as we go.**
(*Wave arms above head.*)	(*Wiggle arms down low.*)

Sign 'n Say

Say: Jesus told stories to help people learn about God's love.

 We can learn about God's love.

Supplies

None

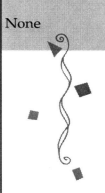

Teach the children the Bible verse, "God is love" (1 John 4:8), using signs from American Sign Language.

God — Point the index finger of your right hand with the other fingers curled down. Bring the hand down and open the palm.

Love — Cross your hands at your wrists and press over your heart.

The Two Houses

by Daphna Flegal

Have the children bring their storybooks (**Reproducibles 9A and 9B**) *and sit down in your story area.*

Say: Jesus told stories to help people learn about God's love. The stories Jesus told are called parables. Say the word *parable* **with me.**

Jesus told a story about two houses.

(Have the children turn to the first page in their storybooks.)

The wise man built his house on rock. Point to the picture of the house. *(Have the children put a finger on the picture of the house.)* Now point to the picture of the rock. *(Have the children put a finger on the picture of the rock.)*

(Have the children turn to the second page in their storybooks.)

One day it began to rain. It rained and rained. It rained so hard that there were floods all around the house. The winds began to blow. The water from the rains and the flood beat upon the house.

Let's make the sound of the wind and rain. *(Have the children sit their storybooks down. Show the children how to rub their palms together to make the sound of rain. Have the children blow to make the sound of the wind.)*

But the house did not fall because it had been built on rock.

(Have the children turn to the third page in their storybooks.)

The foolish man built his house on sand. Point to the picture of the house. *(Have the children put a finger on the picture of the house.)* Now point to the picture of the sand. *(Have the children put a finger on the picture of the sand.)*

(Have the children turn to the fourth page in their storybooks.)

One day it began to rain. It rained and rained. It rained so hard that there were floods all around the house. The winds began to blow. The water from the rains and the flood beat upon the house.

Let's make the sound of the wind and rain. *(Have the children sit their storybooks down. Show the children how to rub their palms together to make the sound of rain. Have the children blow to make the sound of the wind.)*

The house built on the sand — FELL DOWN! *(Slap hands on the floor.)*

Jesus told this story to help people learn about God's love. When we show people God's love, we are like the wise man who built his house on the rock.

Bible Verse Fun

Choose a child to hold the Bible open to 1 John 4:8.

Say: Today our Bible story is a story Jesus told about two houses. Jesus told the story to help people learn about God's love. We can learn about God's love.

We can learn about God's love.

Say the Bible verse, "God is love" (1 John 4:8), for the children. Have the children say the Bible verse after you.

Help the children learn the Bible verse by singing. Sing the words printed below to the tune of "The Wheels on the Bus."

> The Bible tells us "God is love."
> "God is love, God is love."
> The Bible tells us "God is love."
> Let's share God's love.
> © 1998 Abingdon Press

Play a game with the children to reinforce the Bible verse. Give each child a piece of scrap paper. Have the children crumple their paper into balls and then place their paper balls on the floor. Be sure there is space to move between each ball.

Say: Jesus told a story about two houses. The wise man built his house upon a rock. Let's pretend our paper balls are rocks. Stand next to your pretend rock and do what I tell you to do:

Put one finger on your rock.
Touch your knee to your rock.
Say the Bible verse, "God is love" (1 John 4:8).
Put your elbow on your rock.
March around your rock.
Say the Bible verse, "God is love" (1 John 4:8).
Tiptoe around your rock.
Sit down beside your rock.
Say the Bible verse, "God is love" (1 John 4:8).
Put your ear on your rock.
Touch the rock with your toes.
Say the Bible verse, "God is love" (1 John 4:8).
Hop over your rock.
Pick up your rock and throw it away.

Supplies

None

Sing!

Have the children move to an open area of the room.

Say: Today our Bible story is a story Jesus told about two houses. Jesus told this story to help people learn about God's love.

Sing the song "Jesus Taught" to the tune of "London Bridge." Encourage the children to follow your motions.

Jesus Taught
(Tune: "London Bridge")

Jesus taught about God's love,
(Fold your hands over your heart.)
Clap your hand; shout hurray!
(Clap your hands; jab hand in the air.)
Jesus taught about God's love,
(Fold your hands over your heart.)
God is love.

Jesus taught about God's love,
(Fold your hands over your heart.)
Stomp your feet; shout hurray!
(Stomp your feet; jab hand in the air.)
Jesus taught about God's love,
(Fold your hands over your heart.)
God is love.

Supplies

storybooks from "Storybook Sashay" activity (Reproducibles 9A and 9B), newspaper, smocks, sponge paintbrushes, tempera paint, shallow tray, construction paper, scissors, stapler and staples

House Painting

Cover the work area with newspaper and have the children wear paint smocks to protect their clothing. Pour tempera paint into shallow trays. Cut a piece of construction paper in half for each child. Give each child the two half-sheets of construction paper. Write the children's names on their papers.

Say: Our storybooks show the story Jesus told about two houses. Let's make a cover for our storybook.

Give each child a sponge paintbrush. Let the children use the brushes to paint on their construction paper. Set the papers aside to dry.

Say: Jesus told a story about two houses to help people learn about God's love.

> ## We can learn about God's love.

When the house prints are dry, place one page at the front of the storybook and one page at the back of the storybook to make front and back covers. Staple the covers to the storybook on the left-hand side.

Love Lessons

Supplies

None

Have the children sit down in your story area. Show the children how to sign the Bible verse again (see page 93).

Say: We can learn many things about God's love. We know that God is love. I will tell you something that we can learn about God's love. Then I want you to sign the Bible verse with me, "God is love" (1 John 4:8).

God loves everyone.
God is love. (*Sign the verse.*)
We show love when we help our moms and dads.
God is love. (*Sign the verse.*)

God wants us to show love to others.
God is love. (*Sign the verse.*)
We show love when we pray for one another.
God is love. (*Sign the verse.*)
We show love when we share toys.
God is love. (*Sign the verse.*)

Parable Prayers

Supplies

construction paper, scissors

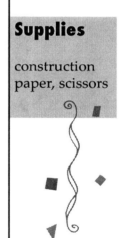

Cut out a large heart from construction paper.

Have the children sit in a circle. Show the children the heart.

Say: One way we show love is by praying. Let's pray for one another.

Give the first child in the circle the heart.

Pray: Thank you, God, for (*child's name*) and (*her or his*) friend, (*name of child sitting next to first child named*). Amen.

Have the child holding the heart repeat the prayer for the friend: Thank you, God, for (*name of child sitting next to him or her*).

Have the child pass the heart to the next child. Repeat until every child has had a turn passing the heart and praying.

REPRODUCIBLE 9A

The Sower

Bible Verse

God is love.

1 John 4:8

Bible Story

Matthew 13:3-9, 18-23

The parable of the sower is a good example of Jesus' use of the familiar to make a point with his listeners. Agriculture was a major business in Galilee, and sowing seed would have been a common experience or at least a common sight for Jesus' hearers.

Farmers owned grainfields adjacent to their neighbors' with boundaries marked only by a pile of stones. After preparing the soil by plowing it once if they thought it needed plowing, they would scatter fistfuls of seed over it with sweeping arm motions as they walked its length and breadth. Finally, they would plow a second time (or in some cases the first time) to cover the seed with dirt.

Inevitably as the seed was scattered, some of it would fall beyond the boundaries of the field, perhaps on a well-worn path at the field's edge or in soil that had not been prepared because it lay in a thin layer over rock. Jesus told his disciples that the various kinds of soil in his story represented the circumstances of those to whom the word of God was preached. Those who were represented by seed growing in good soil were those who hear God's word and acted on it. Good seed were persons who knew and understood God's love, and shared it with others.

The parable had a surprise ending for Jesus' listeners. The yields he suggested were far beyond the fifteenfold yield that would have been considered excellent in those times. Thus he was placing great value on hearing and obeying God's word.

When we know and understand God's love for us, we will share it with others. We become like seed in good soil. Help your children see how they can share God's love by being kind, by praying for others, and by being helpful at home, at church, and at other places.

We can share God's love with others.

If time is limited, we recommend those activities that are noted in **boldface**. Depending on your time and the number of children, you may be able to include more activities.

ACTIVITY	TIME	SUPPLIES	
How Does Your Garden Grow?	15 minutes	Reproducible 10A, scissors, crayons, construction paper, glue	JOIN THE FUN
Parable Parade	5 minutes	None	BIBLE STORY FUN
Sign 'n Say	5 minutes	None	
Bible Story: Seeds	**10 minutes**	**None**	
Bible Verse Fun	**10 minutes**	**Bible**	
Sing!	5 minutes	None	
Seeds to Share	10 minutes	Reproducible 10B, crayons, tape, seed packets (one per child)	
Go 'n Grow	5 minutes	None	LIVE THE FUN
Parable Prayers	**5 minutes**	**construction paper, scissors**	

Supplies

Reproducible 10A, scissors, crayons, construction paper, glue

How Does Your Garden Grow?

Photocopy and cut apart the flower growth cards **(Reproducible 10A)** for each child. Mix the cards out of order. Have the children place the cards in the correct sequence to show how a flower grows. Talk with the children about the pictures.

Say: Today our Bible story is a story Jesus told about a farmer who was planting seeds and about how the seeds grew. Jesus told this story to help people understand that God loves us and wants us to share God's love with others.

We can share God's love with others.

Let the children color the pictures with crayons. Give each child a piece of construction paper. Let the children glue the cards on the construction paper in the correct sequence.

When the children are finished with their pictures, say the following action poem and have the children do the motions.

> **Farmer, farmer, tell me, please,**
> *(Shake finger.)*
> **How does your garden grow?**
> *(Put hands on hips.)*
>
> **First I plant the tiny seeds**
> *(Pretend to plant seeds in the ground.)*
> **And water them just so.**
> *(Pretend to pour water on the seeds.)*
> **Then I hope the sun will shine**
> *(Hold arms in circle over head.)*
> **To help them grow and grow!**
> *(Crouch down, then stretch up on tiptoes.)*
>
> **Farmer, farmer, tell me, please,**
> *(Shake finger.)*
> **How does your garden grow?**
> *(Put hands on hips.)*

Parable Parade

Say: The stories Jesus told are called parables. Let's say the word *parable.* (*Have the children repeat it.*) **Let's have a parable parade.**

Use the following movement poem to lead your children to the story area.

Let's have a parable parade
(*March around the room.*)
And wave our arms up high.
(*Wave arms above head.*)
Let's have a parable parade
(*March around the room.*)
And try to reach the sky.
(*Wave arms above head.*)

Let's have a story stomp
(*Stomp around the room.*)
And wave our arms down low.
(*Wave arms down low.*)
Let's have a story stomp
(*Stomp around the room.*)
And wiggle as we go.
(*Wiggle arms down low.*)

Supplies

None

Sign 'n Say

Say: Jesus told stories to help people learn about God's love.

We can share God's love with others.

Supplies

None

Teach the children the Bible verse, "God is love" (1 John 4:8), using signs from American Sign Language.

God — Point the index finger of your right hand with the other fingers curled down. Bring the hand down and open the palm.

Love — Cross your hands at your wrists and press over your heart.

 **Bible Story**

Seeds

by Daphna Flegal

Have the children sit down in your story area. Tell the children the story. Have the children stand and do the motions for the repeating refrain. Then have the children sit down again.

One day Jesus walked to the seashore. He sat down beside the sea. Many people came to listen to Jesus teach about God. Soon there were so many people that no one could see Jesus. Jesus got into a boat floating on the water. Jesus sat in the boat while all the people stood on the seashore. Now the people could see Jesus. While Jesus was sitting in the boat, he told the people a story about a farmer and some seeds.

A farmer went into his field
To plant seeds in the ground.
He threw seeds here.
(Pretend to throw seeds with one arm in a wide, sweeping motion.)
He threw seeds there.
(Pretend to throw seeds with your other arm in a wide, sweeping motion.)
He threw seeds all around.
(Hold out both arms and turn around.)

Some seeds fell on the road. Birds saw the seeds. They flew down and ate the seeds up.

A farmer went into his field
To plant seeds in the ground.
He threw seeds here.
(Pretend to throw seeds with one arm in a wide, sweeping motion.)
He threw seeds there.
(Pretend to throw seeds with your other arm in a wide, sweeping motion.)
He threw seeds all around.
(Hold out both arms and turn around.)

Some seeds fell among the rocks where there was not much dirt. Plants grew from these seeds, but there was not enough dirt to grow healthy roots. When the sun shone down on the plants, the plants got too hot and died.

A farmer went into his field
To plant seeds in the ground.
He threw seeds here.
(Pretend to throw seeds with one arm in a wide sweeping motion.)
He threw seeds there.
(Pretend to throw seeds with other arm in a wide sweeping motion.)
He threw seeds all around.
(Hold out both arms and turn around.)

Some seed fell among thorns. The plants grew, but the thorns grew faster. Soon the thorns choked the plants, and the plants died.

A farmer went into his field
To plant seeds in the ground.
He threw seeds here.
(Pretend to throw seeds with one arm in a wide, sweeping motion.)
He threw seeds there.
(Pretend to throw seeds with your other arm in a wide, sweeping motion.)
He threw seeds all around.
(Hold out both arms and turn around.)

Some seed fell on good dirt. Many plants grew from the seeds. They grew and grew and grew!

Jesus told this story to help people understand that God loves us and wants us to share God's love with others.

Bible Verse Fun

Choose a child to hold the Bible open to 1 John 4:8.

Say: Today our Bible story is a story Jesus told about a farmer who was planting seeds and about how the seeds grew. Jesus told this story to help people understand that God loves us and wants us to share God's love with others.

We can share God's love with others.

Say the Bible verse, "God is love" (1 John 4:8), for the children. Have the children say the Bible verse after you.

Help the children learn the Bible verse by singing. Sing the words printed below to the tune of "The Wheels on the Bus."

> The Bible tells us "God is love."
> "God is love, God is love."
> The Bible tells us "God is love."
> Let's share God's love.
> © 1998 Abingdon Press

Play a game with the children to reinforce the Bible verse. Have the children sit in a circle in an open area of the room for a game similar to "Duck, Duck, Goose."

Choose one child to be "IT." Have IT move around the outside of the circle and lightly tap each child on the head as he or she says the Bible verse: **God** *(tap)* **is** *(tap)* **love** *(tap)*.

The child tapped on the word "love" chases IT around the circle to the empty spot. This child becomes IT.

Continue the game until each child has an opportunity to be IT.

▲ BIBLE STORY FUN

Supplies

None

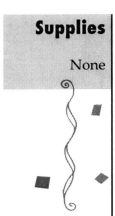

Sing!

Have the children move to an open area of the room.

Say: Today our Bible story is a story Jesus told about a farmer who was planting seeds and about how the seeds grew. Jesus told this story to help people understand that God loves us and wants us to share God's love with others.

Sing the song "God Loves Us" to the tune of "Hot Cross Buns." Encourage the children to follow your motions. Sing the song several times.

God Loves Us
(Tune: "Hot Cross Buns")

God loves me.
(Point to self.)
God loves you.
(Point to others.)
We can share God's love with others.
(Shake a friend's hand.)
God loves us.
(Hug self.)

Supplies

Reproducible 10B, crayons, tape, seed packets (one per child)

Seeds to Share

Photocopy the sunflower card **(Reproducible 10B)** for each child. Let the children decorate the sunflower on the cards with crayons.

Show each child how to fold the bottom of the card up so that the fold forms a pocket. Tape each side of the pocket together.

Then show each child how to fold the card along the center fold. The sunflower should be on the cover of the card, and the pocket should be inside the card.

Give each child a seed packet. Help each child place the seed packet inside the pocket. Secure the packet with tape.

Say: Jesus told a story about a farmer who was planting seeds and about how the seeds grew to help people understand that God loves us and wants us to share God's love with others. We can share God's love with others. One way we can share love is by sending cards. Give your card to a friend to tell him or her about God's love.

Go 'n Grow

Have the children sit on the floor in a line. Go to the first child and say the poem printed below.

(Child's name), (child's name),
**come with me,
And we'll share
God's love, you see.
For when we share
with friends we know,
We're helping God's love
grow and grow.**

Have the child hook on behind you as if you were making a train. Lead the child around the room and repeat "grow and grow" over and over.

Then go back to the children waiting in line. Say the poem again to the next child and have that child hook onto the back of the first child. Repeat until everyone has joined the train.

Parable Prayers

Cut out a large heart from construction paper.

Have the children sit in a circle. Show the children the heart.

Say: One way we show love is by praying. Let's pray for each other.

Give the first child in the circle the heart.

Pray: Thank you, God, for *(child's name)* **and** *(her or his)* **friend,** *(name of child sitting next to first child named).* **Amen.**

Have the child holding the heart repeat the prayer for the friend: **Thank you, God, for** *(name of child sitting next to him or her).*

Have the child pass the heart to the next child. Repeat until every child has had a turn passing the heart and praying.

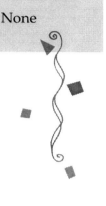

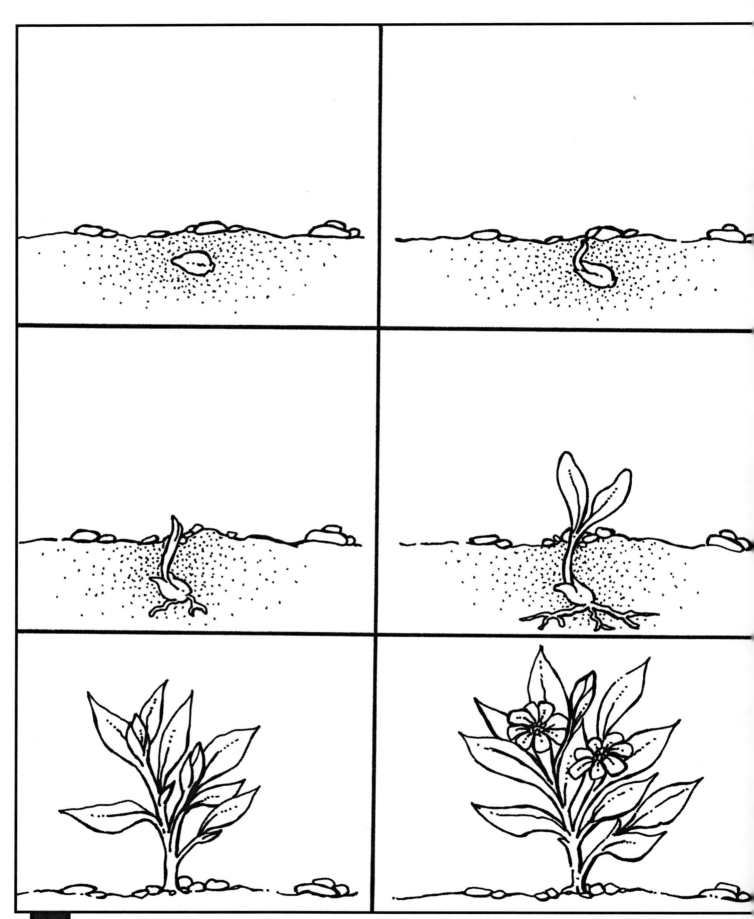

REPRODUCIBLE **10A**

God is love.
1 John 4:8

The Good Samaritan

Bible Verse

Love your neighbor as you love yourself.

Luke 10:27, GNT

Bible Story

Luke 10:25-37

Some of the religious leaders of Jesus' day were always trying to ask him questions that would trip him up. On this occasion someone asked him, "What must I do to have eternal life?" Jesus pointed out that the man already had the answer. As a practicing Jew he would have recited the law twice a day, "Love the Lord your God with all your heart, with all your soul, with all your strength, and with all your mind; and love your neighbor as you love yourself" (Luke 10:27, GNT).

Not to be outdone the man asked another question, "Just who is my neighbor?" Jesus carefully selected the setting and the character of the parable to answer the question. The journey from Jerusalem to Jericho was one filled with danger. Along the rocky, rugged terrain robbers found many places to hide. Sometimes one robber would lie alongside the road pretending to be ill while his friends lay in wait to pounce on anyone who stopped to offer help.

It may be that this is what went though the minds of the Levite and the priest as they passed the injured traveler, or it may have been their reluctance to risk touching a dead man and having to give up serving in the Temple because they were unclean.

Jesus' listeners must have been astonished to hear that a Samaritan came to the aid of the injured man. They more likely would have expected the traveler to meet his death at the hands of the Samaritan, a people despised by the Jews. The involvement of such a character gave the definition of "neighbor" new meaning. Anyone is our neighbor. The love of God calls us to express our love to neighbors near and far.

Preschoolers may have trouble with the concept of neighbors around the world, but they can understand concrete ways of helping others.

We can be good neighbors.

If time is limited, we recommend those activities that are noted in **boldface**. Depending on your time and the number of children, you may be able to include more activities.

ACTIVITY	TIME	SUPPLIES
Set the Stage	**10 Minutes**	**Reproducibles 11A and 11B, drinking straws or craft sticks, scissors, crayons, tape or glue, box large enough for the background picture to fit inside**
Jericho Jog	10 minutes	newspaper or other scrap paper, masking tape
Parable Parade	5 minutes	None
Neighbor, Neighbor	5 minutes	chair
Bible Story: The Good Neighbor	**10 minutes**	**theater box and storytelling figures (Reproducibles 11A and 11B)**
Bible Verse Fun	**5 minutes**	**Bible**
Sing!	5 minutes	None
Who's My Neighbor?	5 minutes	None
First Aid Patrol	10 minutes	Reproducible 11B, scissors, crayons or markers, box with lid, plain wrapping paper or paper bag, tape, glue, first-aid kit supplies (adhesive bandages, first aid cream, gauze, and so forth)
Parable Prayers	**5 minutes**	**construction paper, scissors**

JOIN THE FUN

BIBLE STORY FUN

LIVE THE FUN

Supplies

Reproducibles 11A and 11B, drinking straws or craft sticks, scissors, crayons, tape or glue, box large enough for the background picture to fit inside

Set the Stage

Photocopy the background picture **(Reproducible 11A)** and the storytelling figures **(Reproducible 11B)**. Let the children work together to make a puppet theatre. Have the children decorate the picture and storytelling figures with crayons. When the children have finished coloring, cut out the storytelling figures. Tape or glue a drinking straw or craft stick on the back of each storytelling figure so that the straws or sticks come up from the figures' heads.

Cut the flaps from the box or remove the box lid. Let the children decorate the box with crayons. Glue or tape the background picture onto the inside of a box. Set the box and storytelling figures in your story area.

Say: Today our Bible story is a story Jesus told about a man who was a good neighbor. The story has a man who was traveling down the road to a town called Jericho. (*Show the children the road on the background picture, and the traveler picture.*) **The story also has robbers,** (*Show robbers picture.*) **a priest,** (*Show priest picture.*) **a leader from the Temple,** (*Show Levite picture.*) **and a Samaritan.** (*Show Samaritan picture.*) **One of these men was a good neighbor to the man who was traveling. Jesus told the story to help people understand that they can be good neighbors and can help one another.**

We can be good neighbors.

Supplies

newspaper or other scrap paper, masking tape

Jericho Jog

Say: The story begins with a man traveling down the road. The road was very rocky. Let's make the rocky road to Jericho.

Give each child a piece of newspaper or other scrap paper. Show the children how to crumple the paper into a ball. Use a loop of tape to secure each paper rock to the floor. Tape the rocks about 18 inches apart to make a road around the room. Have the children line up at the beginning of the rocky road.

Say: Let's pretend we are traveling along the rocky road to Jericho. Let's hop over the rocks as we go.

Have each child hop over each rock to the end of the road. Repeat the game and let the children walk in a circle around each rock.

Parable Parade

Supplies

None

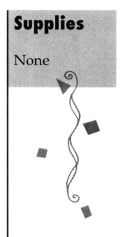

Say: The stories Jesus told are called parables. Let's say the word *parable.* *(Have the children repeat it.)* **Let's have a parable parade.**

Use the following movement poem to lead your children to the story area.

Let's have a parable parade
(March around the room.)
And wave our arms up high.
(Wave arms above head.)
Let's have a parable parade
(March around the room.)
And try to reach the sky.
(Wave arms above head.)

Let's have a story stomp
(Stomp around the room.)
And wave our arms down low.
(Wave arms down low.)
Let's have a story stomp
(Stomp around the room.)
And wiggle as we go.
(Wiggle arms down low.)

Neighbor, Neighbor

Supplies

chair

Say: Jesus told a story to teach people to love their neighbors. He did not mean just the people who live next door, but anyone who needs help. We are all neighbors.

We can be good neighbors.

Place a chair in front of the children. Choose one child to begin the game. Have the child sit down in the chair and cover her or his eyes with both hands. Choose another child to move very quietly and stand behind the chair.

Say: Neighbor, neighbor, who's your neighbor?

Have the child standing behind the chair say, "I'm your neighbor!" and then the Bible verse, "Love your neighbor as you love yourself" (Luke 10:27, GNT). Encourage the child to disguise his or her voice.

Have the child sitting in the chair try to guess who is speaking. Continue the game until everyone has a chance to play.

The Good Neighbor

by Daphna Flegal

*Use the background picture **(Reproducible 11A)** and the storytelling figures **(Reproducible 11B)** as you tell the story to the children (see "Set the Stage," page 112). Place the box theatre where all the children can see the background. Hold each storytelling figure by the straw or stick and follow the directions on the cue sheet as you tell the story using the puppet script.*

Puppet Script	**Cue Sheet**
Jesus told the people this story: Once there was a man traveling down the road to a town called Jericho.	*Move the traveler figure across the front of the background picture.*
Suddenly robbers jumped out from behind some rocks. The robbers hurt the man and took all the man's money. Then the robbers left the man and ran away.	*Quickly bring out the robbers figure. Quickly move the robbers out of sight. Lay the traveler figure down in front of the background.*
Soon a priest came walking down the road. He saw the hurt man. He knew that the man needed help, but he was afraid. The priest crossed the road and hurried by the hurt man. He did not stop to help.	*Move priest figure across the front. Stop priest figure near hurt man. Make priest figure tremble. Quickly move priest figure out of sight.*
Later another leader from the Temple came walking down the road. He saw the hurt man, but he crossed the road and hurried by the hurt man. He did not stop to help.	*Move Levite figure across the front. Stop Levite figure near hurt man. Quickly move Levite figure out of sight.*
Then a third man came riding down the road on his donkey. He was called a Samaritan. When he saw the hurt man he stopped to help. He put the hurt man on his donkey and took him to a place where he could rest and get better. The Samaritan even paid for the hurt man's care.	*Move Samaritan figure across the front. Stop Samaritan figure near hurt man. Pick up traveler figure and slowly move together with Samaritan figure out of sight.*
Jesus finished the story and looked at the people.	
"Three men saw the hurt man on the road," said Jesus. "Who was the neighbor to the man who was hurt?"	*Encourage children to answer the question.*

Bible Verse Fun

Choose a child to hold the Bible open to Luke 10:27.

Say: Today our Bible story is a story Jesus told about a man who was a good neighbor. Jesus told the story to help people understand that they can be good neighbors and can help one another.

We can be good neighbors.

Say the Bible verse, "Love your neighbor as you love yourself" (Luke 10:27, GNT), for the children. Have the children say the Bible verse after you.

Help the children learn the Bible verse by singing. Sing the words printed below to the tune of "This is the Way."

> This is the way to love your neighbor,
> love your neighbor, love your neighbor.
> This is the way to love your neighbor,
> as you love yourself.

Play a game with the children to reinforce the Bible verse. Have the children sit down on the rug or floor.

Say: I'm thinking of my neighbor. My neighbor has *(name something about a child in your class)*. **Who is my neighbor?**

Let the children guess which child you are thinking of. Keep giving clues until the children can guess correctly. Have the child you were describing stand.

Say: Neighbor *(child's name)*, **lead us as we say the Bible verse together.**

Have all the children say the Bible verse as the child is standing. Then have the child sit back down.

Continue the game until you have described each child and had the child stand to lead the Bible verse.

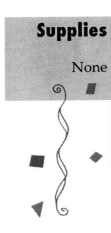

Supplies

None

Sing!

Say: Jesus told a story about a man who was a good neighbor. We can be good neighbors.

Have the children move to an open area of the room. Play the song "Good Neighbors" to the tune of "Boom Boom!"

Good Neighbors
(Tune: "Boom Boom!")

Clap, clap! *(Clap hands.)*
We can all be good neighbors.
Clap, clap! *(Clap hands.)*
We can all be good neighbors.
Lovin' our friends just like
ourselves.
Clap, clap! *(Clap hands.)*
We can all be good neighbors.

Shake, shake! *(Shake hands.)*
We can all be good neighbors.
Shake, shake! *(Shake hands.)*
We can all be good neighbors.
Lovin' our friends just like
ourselves.
Shake, shake! *(Shake hands.)*
We can all be good neighbors.

Stomp, stomp! *(Stomp feet.)*
We can all be good neighbors.
Stomp, stomp! *(Stomp feet.)*
We can all be good neighbors.
Lovin' our friends just like
ourselves.
Stomp, stomp! *(Stomp feet.)*
We can all be good neighbors.

Bump, bump! *(Bump hips with a friend.)*
We can all be good neighbors.
Bump, bump! *(Bump hips with a friend.)*
We can all be good neighbors.
Lovin' our friends just like
ourselves.
Bump, bump! *(Bump hips with a friend.)*
We can all be good neighbors.

Supplies

None

Who's My Neighbor?

Say: Jesus told a story to teach us to love our neighbors. He did not mean just the people who live next door, but anyone who needs help. Listen as I name different people. If the people I name are our neighbors, wave your hands over your head and shout, "Love your neighbor as you love yourself."

The pastor of our church.
Children shout: **Love your neighbor as you love yourself.**
The people who are in the hospital.
Children shout: **Love your neighbor as you love yourself.**
The people who sing in the church choir.
Children shout: **Love your neighbor as you love yourself.**
The people who need food to eat.
Children shout: **Love your neighbor as you love yourself.**
The children in your Sunday school class.
Children shout: **Love your neighbor as you love yourself.**

First Aid Patrol

Supplies

Reproducible 11B, scissors, crayons or markers, box with lid, plain wrapping paper or paper bag, tape, glue, first-aid kit supplies (adhesive bandages, first aid cream, gauze, and so forth)

Photocopy and cut out a set of the storytelling figures (**Reproducible 11B**). Copy enough figures for each child to have one.

Say: Jesus told a story about being a good neighbor. The Samaritan was the good neighbor. He helped the man who was hurt. We can help others.

 We can be good neighbors.

Let's make a first-aid kit to help (*name whatever group you will give the first-aid kit to: the nursery room, a homeless shelter, the church office, or a Mother's Day Out program*).

Show the children the box you have provided. Let the children help you wrap the box with plain paper or with paper cut from a paper bag. Let the children decorate the box with crayons or markers. Give each child a story-telling figure. Let the children color the figures with crayons. Have the children glue the figures onto the outside of the box.

Show the children the items you have purchased to go inside the first-aid kit. Place the items in the box and secure the box lid. If possible, take the children to deliver the first-aid kit.

Parable Prayers

Cut out a large heart from construction paper.

Have the children sit in a circle. Show the children the heart.

Say: One way we can be a good neighbor is by praying. Let's pray for each other.

Give the first child in the circle the heart.

Pray: Thank you, God, for (*child's name*) **and** (*her or his*) **friend,** (*name of child sitting next to first child named*). **Amen.**

Have the child holding the heart repeat the prayer for the friend: **Thank you, God, for** (*name of child sitting next to him or her*).

Have the child pass the heart to the next child. Repeat until every child has had a turn passing the heart and praying.

Supplies

construction paper, scissors

REPRODUCIBLE 11A

Priest

Samaritan

Robbers

Levite

Traveler

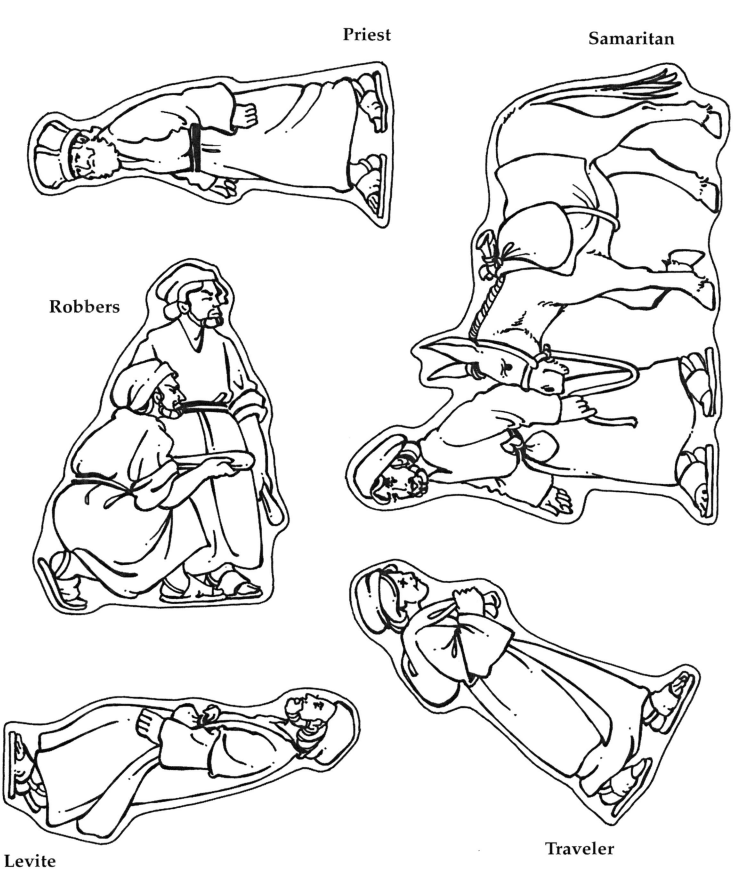

REPRODUCIBLE 11B

The Lost Sheep

Bible Verse

God cares for you.

1 Peter 5:7, CEV

Bible Story

Luke 15:3-7

Jesus' teachings struck a chord with tax collectors, people of lowly birth, and others who were not held in high esteem by the upperclass Jews. The religious leaders of the day rebuked Jesus for the company he kept. In response he told them a series of parables about the lost and the found.

The shepherd who has a hundred sheep, Jesus said, would not rest if even one were lost. Rather, he searched for it until he found it, joyfully laid it on his shoulders, and carried it home. Once there he called his friends to come and share in his joy.

The parallel Jesus drew was very clear. Throughout this entire chapter there runs a single note—one of joy. God rejoices at the return of a sinner to the faith, just as the shepherd rejoices when a lost sheep is once again safe in the fold. Here Jesus is clearly focusing attention on God as a loving parent—only such a God would rejoice in that way.

Children understand what it means to be cared for. Parents and grandparents care for them by feeding and clothing them and providing safe, secure places for them to grow and live. But for preschoolers God's care may be somewhat more difficult to understand unless it is put in concrete terms like the story of the shepherd and his sheep.

Remember that many children today have never seen real sheep, and few have had any experience with shepherds. Help the children understand the importance of the caretaker to those for whom he is caring. Children may relate to caring for a pet at home, or perhaps you could bring a classroom pet to care for over several weeks. Help the children see a relationship between the way they care for animals, the way the shepherd cared for his sheep, and finally how God cares for us in a similar way.

God loves us and cares for us.

If time is limited, we recommend those activities that are noted in **boldface**. Depending on your time and the number of children, you may be able to include more activities.

ACTIVITY	TIME	SUPPLIES	
Fuzzy Wuzzy Was . . .	15 minutes	**Reproducible 12A; scissors; crayons, cotton balls, or packing peanuts; glue; construction paper; tape**	JOIN THE FUN
Parable Parade	5 minutes	None	BIBLE STORY FUN
Sign 'n Say	5 minutes	None	
Bible Story: Little Sheep	10 minutes	**Reproducibles 12A and 12B, scissors, tape, box lid or cookie sheet**	
Bible Verse Fun	5 minutes	**Bible, sheep figure (Reproducible 12A)**	
Five-Fingered Fun	5 minutes	None	
Handy Sheep	10 minutes	black construction paper, safety scissors, cotton balls, glue sticks	LIVE THE FUN
Parable Prayers	5 minutes	**construction paper, scissors**	

Supplies

Reproducible 12A; scissors; crayons, cotton balls, or packing peanuts; glue; construction paper; tape

Fuzzy Wuzzy Was . . .

Photocopy and cut out the sheep mask **(Reproducible 12A)** for each child. Let the children decorate the masks by coloring with crayons, by gluing on cotton balls, or by gluing on packing peanuts.

Cut a two-inch wide strip from construction paper for each child. Tape the head strip to one side of the mask. Have each child hold the mask up to his or her face while you measure the strip around the back of the child's head. Tape the strip to the other side of the mask so that the mask will stay on the child's head.

Say: Jesus told a story about a shepherd and a lost sheep. The shepherd took care of the sheep and loved the sheep. God is like the shepherd.

God loves us and cares for us.

Encourage the children to move around the room and to pretend to be sheep. Allow the children time to pretend.

Say: Come, little sheep, follow me. I am your shepherd.

(Lead the children around the room. Stop in one corner of the room.)

Say: Come and eat, little sheep, eat the sweet-tasting grass.

(Lead the children to another area of the room.)

Say: Come and drink, little sheep, drink the cool water from the stream.

(Lead the children to a rug or to your story area.)

Say: Now rest, little sheep, lie down and sleep in the warm sun.

*(While the children are quiet; **say** the following poem:)*

Fuzzy Wuzzy was a . . . sheep,
He ate grass all day.
He drank water from the stream
Then he'd run and play.

One day Fuzzy wandered off,
And he did not know where.
Fuzzy was afraid and lost,
Far from his shepherd's care.

The shepherd looked for Fuzzy
All day and all night long.
Finally, when he found the sheep,
He sang a happy song.

"Rejoice with me, my sheep was lost,
But now my sheep is found.
Fuzzy Wuzzy is back home.
My sheep are safe and sound."

Parable Parade

Say: The stories Jesus told are called parables. Let's say the word *parable.* *(Have the children repeat it.)* **Let's have a parable parade.**

Use the following movement poem to lead your children to the story area.

> **Let's have a parable parade**
> *(March around the room.)*
> **And wave our arms up high.**
> *(Wave arms above head.)*
> **Let's have a parable parade**
> *(March around the room.)*
> **And try to reach the sky.**
> *(Wave arms above head.)*
>
> **Let's have a story stomp**
> *(Stomp around the room.)*
> **And wave our arms down low.**
> *(Wave arms down low.)*
> **Let's have a story stomp**
> *(Stomp around the room.)*
> **And wiggle as we go.**
> *(Wiggle arms down low.)*

Sign 'n Say

Teach the children the Bible verse, "God cares for you" (1 Peter 5:7, CEV), using signs from American Sign Language.

God — Point the index finger of your right hand with the other fingers curled down. Bring the hand down and open the palm.

Cares — Alternate moving palms from you the forehead level down.

You — Point out with your index finger.

God

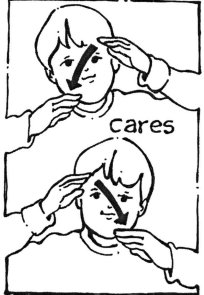
cares

you

Supplies

None

Supplies

None

Little Sheep

by Daphna Flegal

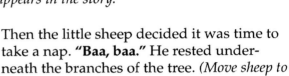

Photocopy the background picture **(Reproducible 12B)**. *Tape the background picture on a box lid or cookie sheet. Photocopy and cut out the sheep and shepherd figures* **(Reproducible 12A)**. *Fold the tabs on each figure to make the figure stand. Hold the background picture where the children can see it.*

Have the children repeat the "Baa, baa" each time it appears in the story.

Jesus told a story about a shepherd and his sheep. The shepherd took care of his sheep. *(Place the shepherd figure on the background.)*

The shepherd took his sheep to the hillside to eat the sweet-tasting grass. *(Move the shepherd to grassy area.)* While the sheep were eating, the shepherd counted his sheep. Ninety-eight. Ninety-nine. One hundred.

The shepherd took his sheep to drink water from the stream. *(Move shepherd to stream.)* While the sheep were drinking, the shepherd counted his sheep. Ninety-eight. Ninety-nine. One hundred.

The shepherd took his sheep to rest under the shade of a tree. *(Move shepherd to tree.)* While the sheep were resting, the shepherd counted his sheep. Ninety-eight. Ninety-nine. Ninety-eight. Ninety-nine! One sheep was missing! The shepherd went to look for his sheep. *(Remove shepherd.)*

(Place the sheep figure on the background.)

One little sheep had wandered off. **"Baa, baa."** First the little sheep played in the cool water of the stream. *(Move sheep to stream.)*

Then the little sheep was hungry. **"Baa, baa."** He ate some of the sweet-tasting grass. *(Move sheep to grassy area.)*

Then the little sheep decided it was time to take a nap. **"Baa, baa."** He rested underneath the branches of the tree. *(Move sheep to tree.)*

While the sheep was napping, a loud noise startled the little sheep. The sheep was afraid! What if the noise was a wolf or a bear? **"Baa, baa!"** The little sheep ran to hide behind a rock. *(Move sheep to rock.)*

The little sheep was still afraid. He wished he had not wandered away from his shepherd. Maybe the rock was not the best hiding place. **"Baa, baa!"** The little sheep ran to a nearby bush. *(Move sheep to bush.)*

The little sheep's wool caught on the branches of the bush. The little sheep was stuck. **"Baa! Baa!"** cried the little sheep.

The shepherd heard the little sheep crying. *(Leave the sheep by the bush; move shepherd to bush.)* He found the little sheep in the bush. He carefully untangled the little sheep's wool from the bush. He picked the sheep up in his arms and carried him back to the other sheep.

"Baa, baa." The little sheep was happy to be with his shepherd. Ninety-eight. Ninety-nine. One hundred! The shepherd counted his sheep. The shepherd was happy that he had found the lost sheep.

Bible Verse Fun

Choose a child to hold the Bible open to 1 Peter 5:7.

Say: Today our Bible story is a story Jesus told about a shepherd and a lost sheep. The shepherd took care of the sheep and loved the sheep. God is like the shepherd. God loves us and cares for us.

God loves us and cares for us.

Say the Bible verse, "God cares for you" (1 Peter 5:7, CEV), for the children. Have the children say the Bible verse after you.

Help the children learn the Bible verse by singing. Sing the words printed below to the tune of "London Bridge."

> The Bible says "God cares for you,
> cares for you, cares for you."
> The Bible says "God cares for you,
> God cares for you."

Play a game with the children to reinforce the Bible verse. Photocopy and cut out the sheep figure **(Reproducible 12A).**

Have the children sit down in your story area. Show the children the sheep figure. Choose one child to be the shepherd. Have the shepherd go with a teacher out of the room or hide his or her eyes with both hands. Hide the sheep figure somewhere in the room.

Have the shepherd come back into the room or uncover her or his eyes. Have the shepherd look for the sheep. When the shepherd is close to the sheep, have the other children baa like sheep. When the shepherd moves away from the sheep, have the children stay quiet.

Have all the children clap their hands when the shepherd finds the lamb. Then have the children repeat the Bible verse together: "God cares for you" (1 Peter 5:7, CEV).

Repeat the game until everyone has an opportunity to be the shepherd.

Say: God is like a shepherd who takes care of the sheep.

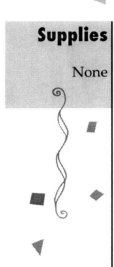

Supplies	# Five-Fingered Fun
None	

Have the children sit down in your story area. Encourage the children to copy your hand movements as you say the following fingerplay.

A shepherd had one hundred sheep.
(Hold up your index finger. Curl other fingers down in palm.)
Ninety-seven, ninety-eight,
(Hold up fifth finger, then fourth finger.)
Ninety-nine, one hundred!
(Hold up third finger, then thumb.)

Ev'ry morning he'd count his sheep.
(Hold up your index finger. Curl other fingers down in palm.)
Ninety-seven, ninety-eight,
(Hold up fifth finger, then fourth finger.)
Ninety-nine, one hundred!
(Hold up third finger, then thumb.)

Ev'ry evening he'd count again.
(Hold up your index finger. Curl other fingers down in palm.)
Ninety-seven, ninety-eight,
(Hold up fifth finger, then fourth finger.)
Ninety-nine, one hundred!
(Hold up third finger, then thumb.)

From number one to ten times ten.
(Hold up your index finger. Curl other fingers down in palm.)
Ninety-seven, ninety-eight,
(Hold up fifth finger, then fourth finger.)
Ninety-nine, one hundred!
(Hold up third finger, then thumb.)

One day he was counting fine,
(Hold up your index finger. Curl other fingers down in palm.)
Ninety-seven, ninety-eight,
(Hold up fifth finger, then fourth finger.)
Ninety-nine . . .
(Hold up third finger. Keep thumb curled in palm.)

"Oh, no!" he said, "only ninety-nine!"
(Hold up your index finger. Curl other fingers down in palm.)
Ninety-seven, ninety-eight,
(Hold up fifth finger, then fourth finger.)
Ninety-nine . . .
(Hold up third finger. Keep thumb curled in palm.)

The shepherd looked high.
(Move hand up.)
The shepherd looked low.
(Move hand down.)
'Til he found the sheep
(Wiggle thumb.)
On the rocks below.
(Hold up thumb.)

"Hurray!" said the shepherd,
(Wiggle hand.)
"Hurray! Hurray!
(Wiggle hand.)
I found the sheep
(Hold up thumb.)
That was lost today."
(Wiggle thumb.)

The shepherd counted the sheep that night.
(Hold up your index finger. Curl other fingers down in palm.)
Ninety-seven, ninety-eight,
(Hold up fifth finger, then fourth finger.)
Ninety-nine, one hundred!
(Hold up third finger, then thumb.)

And that's the number
That was just right!

Handy Sheep

Trace each child's hand on a piece of black construction paper. Keep the fingers spread apart. Help the children cut out their handprints. Turn the handprint so that the four fingers are pointing down to make the legs of the sheep. The thumb will become the sheep's head.

Let the children glue cotton balls onto the palm of the handprint.

Say: Jesus told a story about a shepherd and a lost sheep. The shepherd searched and searched for the sheep until the lost sheep was found. The shepherd loved the sheep. God is like the shepherd.

God loves us and takes care of us.

Parable Prayers

Cut out a large heart from construction paper.

Have the children sit in a circle. Show the children the heart.

Say: We know God loves us and cares for us. Let's say a thank-you prayer to God.

Give the first child in the circle the heart.

Pray: Thank you, God, for (*child's name*) **and** (*her or his*) **friend,** (*name of child sitting next to first child named*). **Amen.**

Have the child holding the heart repeat the prayer for the friend: **Thank you, God, for** (*name of child sitting next to him or her*).

Have the child pass the heart to the next child. Repeat until every child has had a turn passing the heart and praying.

REPRODUCIBLE 12A

ALL–IN–ONE BIBLE FUN

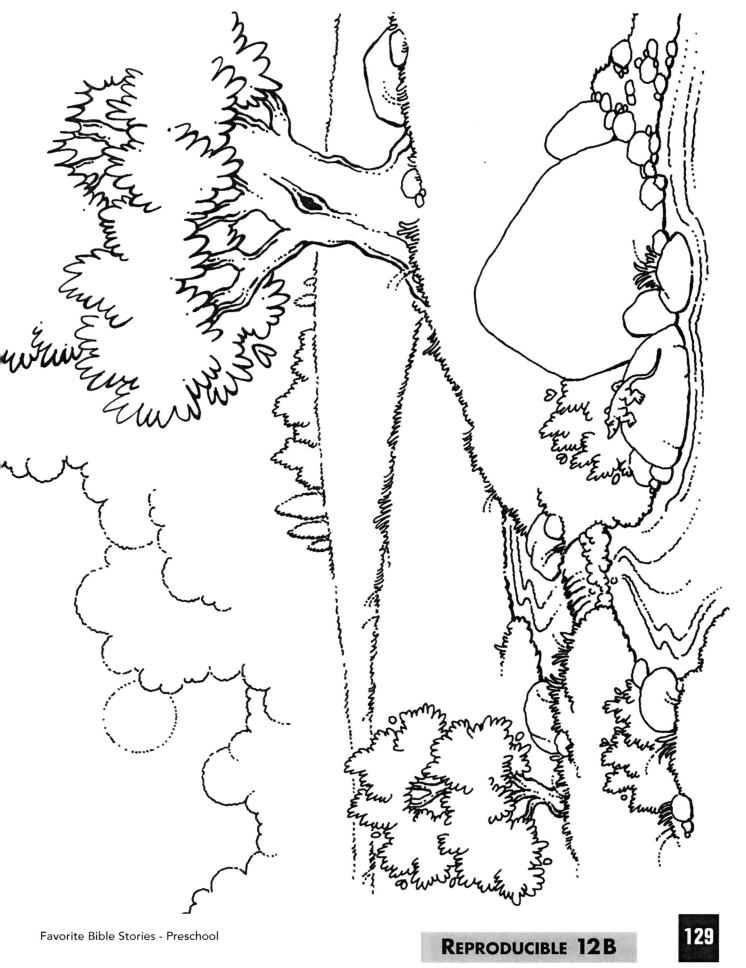

REPRODUCIBLE 12B

All-in-One
BIBLE PRESCHOOL
FUN

The Forgiving Father

Bible Verse

God cares for you.

1 Peter 5:7, CEV

Bible Story

Luke 15:11-32

Jesus didn't make any distinctions between people, and the religious leaders of the day found that hard to understand. Tax collectors, Samaritans, Roman soldiers — weren't these people sinners? Why would Jesus spend so much time with them?

Jesus told several stories so that they might see these people as he did. A lamb, a coin, and a son are all lost and found. Each of the parables has the same message: God rejoices when one of God's children returns to a right way of living, just as we rejoice when we find something we have lost.

The parable of the forgiving father tells of a deliberate choice to "become lost." The youngest of two sons chose to leave the love and security of his father's home. His words and actions caused his father sorrow, but the father let him choose his own course of action.

At first the son had a good time, but soon his money was gone. The only job he could find

was feeding pigs. This would have been degrading for a Bible-times Jew because eating pork was forbidden by Jewish law. Worse, he was so hungry that he contemplated eating the husks he was feeding the pigs.

Desperate for food and shelter, he determined to return to his father and beg him to take him on as a hired servant. But there was no question of that. As soon as the father saw his lost son, he welcomed him home unconditionally.

God's love for each of us must be far greater, even for those who choose to turn away from God. God is always ready and waiting to receive us unconditionally again.

Help children see the parallel between God and a loving parent who is always ready to forgive. Remind children that God loves each of us always — even when we make mistakes.

God always loves us, even when we make mistakes.

If time is limited, we recommend those activities that are noted in **boldface**. Depending on your time and the number of children, you may be able to include more activities.

ACTIVITY	TIME	SUPPLIES
Pig Mania	5 minutes	Reproducible 13A, scissors
This Little Piggy	**15 minutes**	**Reproducible 13B, scissors, crayons, tape or glue**
Parable Parade	5 minutes	None
Sign 'n Say	5 minutes	None
Bible Story: The Loving Father	**10 minutes**	**pig noses from "This Little Piggy" activity (Reproducible 13B)**
Bible Verse Fun	**5 minutes**	**Bible**
Sing!	5 minutes	None
Feed the Pigs	10 minutes	Reproducible 13A, scissors, scrap paper, glue, box with open top or paper grocery bag, optional: plain paper to wrap box
Oops!	10 minutes	None
Parable Prayers	**5 minutes**	**construction paper, scissors**

JOIN THE FUN

BIBLE STORY FUN

LIVE THE FUN

Pig Mania

Photocopy and cut apart at least two copies of the pig pictures (**Reproducible 13A**). Mix up the pictures and place them on a table or rug. Let the children enjoy matching the pictures.

Say: Our Bible story today is a story Jesus told about a father and son. The son made a mistake, but his father still loved him. The pigs have something to do with the mistake the son made. We will find out about the pigs when we hear the Bible story. Jesus told the story to help people understand that God is like a loving parent. God always loves us, even when we make mistakes.

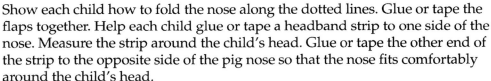
God loves us, even when we make mistakes.

This Little Piggy

Photocopy and cut out the pig noses and headband strip (**Reproducible 13B**) for each child. Give each child a pig nose. Let the children decorate the pig noses with crayons.

Show each child how to fold the nose along the dotted lines. Glue or tape the flaps together. Help each child glue or tape a headband strip to one side of the nose. Measure the strip around the child's head. Glue or tape the other end of the strip to the opposite side of the pig nose so that the nose fits comfortably around the child's head.

Say: Our Bible story today is a story Jesus told about a father and a son. The son made a mistake, but his father still loved him. The pigs have something to do with the mistake the son made. We will find out about the pigs when we hear the Bible story.

Encourage the children to wear their pig noses and to pretend to be pigs. Use the following suggestions to help the children move around the room.

This little piggy said, "Oink, oink, oink."
This little piggy rolled in the mud.
This little piggy ran around the pigpen.
This little piggy ate a big supper.
This little piggy took a nap in the sun.

Parable Parade

Supplies

None

Say: The stories Jesus told are called parables. Let's say the word *parable.* *(Have the children repeat it.)* **Let's have a parable parade.**

Use the following movement poem to lead your children to the story area.

> **Let's have a parable parade**
> *(March around the room.)*
> **And wave our arms up high.**
> *(Wave arms above head.)*
> **Let's have a parable parade**
> *(March around the room.)*
> **And try to reach the sky.**
> *(Wave arms above head.)*
>
> **Let's have a story stomp**
> *(Stomp around the room.)*
> **And wave our arms down low.**
> *(Wave arms down low.)*
> **Let's have a story stomp**
> *(Stomp around the room.)*
> **And wiggle as we go.**
> *(Wiggle arms down low.)*

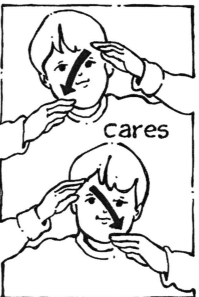

Sign 'n Say

Supplies

None

Teach the children the Bible verse, "God cares for you" (l Peter 5:7, CEV), using signs from American Sign Language.

God — Point the index finger of your right hand with the other fingers curled down. Bring the hand down and open your palm.

Cares — Alternate moving palms from the forehead level down.

You — Point out with your index finger.

The Loving Father

by Susan Isbell

*Encourage the children to wear their pig noses (**Reproducible 13B**) and to join you in your story area.*

Say: Today our Bible story is a story Jesus told about a father and his son. There are also pigs in the story. But the son did not like pigs. Having to take care of pigs made the son feel sad. When you hear me say the word *sad*, pretend to be pigs and say, "Oink, oink." When you hear me say the word *happy*, clap your hands.

Once upon a time there was a man who had two sons whom he loved very much. The two sons made the man very **happy**.

One day the younger son came to the father and said, "I am tired of living at home. Give me my share of the money now. I want to leave home." The father must have felt **sad**, but he gave the younger son the money.

The son was excited. He went to a country far, far away. He spent lots of money! He had lots of fun! He was **happy**!

But soon all his money was gone. He had no money for food. Alone and **sad**, the son finally found a job.

Oink! Oink! His job was feeding pigs. And he hated pigs! He didn't even want to touch the pigs. But he was so hungry, he would have been glad to eat the pigs' food. The son was very **sad**.

The son decided to go home. He wanted to tell his father he was sorry. He hoped his father would give him a job working in the fields. The son went back to his home. As he came near his house, he could not believe what he saw. His father was running down the road to meet him! The son was very **happy**!

"My son!" cried the father. "My son is home!" His father hugged him, kissed him, and welcomed him home. The father was very **happy**.

"Father, I'm sorry," said the son. "I have no money left. I made a mistake. What I did was wrong." The son felt **sad**.

"I love you, and I'm glad you are home," said the father.

The father planned a big party to welcome his son home. The father and the son were **happy**.

Jesus told this story so that people would know that God loves and forgives each of us, even when we make mistakes and do something wrong. Making mistakes can make us sad, but God's love can make us **happy**.

Bible Verse Fun

Choose a child to hold the Bible open to 1 Peter 5:7.

Say: Our Bible story today is a story Jesus told about a father and son. The son made a mistake, but his father still loved him. Jesus told the story to help people understand that God is like a loving parent. God always loves us, even when we make mistakes. God cares about each one of us.

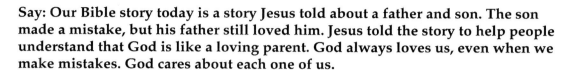

God loves us, even when we make mistakes.

Say the Bible verse, "God cares for you" (1 Peter 5:7, CEV), for the children. Have the children say the Bible verse after you.

Help the children learn the Bible verse by singing. Sing the words printed below to the tune of "London Bridge."

> The Bible says "God cares for you,
> cares for you, cares for you."
> The Bible says "God cares for you,
> God cares for you."
>
> ©1998 Abingdon Press

Play a game like "Mother, May I?" with the children to reinforce the Bible verse. Have the children move to one side of the room. Stand on the other side of the room.

Say: Jesus told a story about a father and son. The son made a mistake, but his father still loved him. Jesus told the story to help people understand that God is like a loving parent.

Choose a child to begin the game.

Say: (Child's name), you may take three baby steps to come home.

Have the child **ask: Father, may I?**

Say: Yes, you may (or no, you may not).

If you say yes, have the child take the steps. If you say no, have the child wait a turn. Continue the game, giving each child turns until the children can touch you. Other suggestions for movement are: take giant steps, jump once, change number of steps, take one step backwards, and so forth.

When the children arrive at "home," **say: Welcome home! "God cares for you"** (1 Peter 5:7, CEV).

▲ BIBLE STORY FUN

Supplies

None

Sing!

Have the children move to an open area of the room.

Say: Our Bible story today is a story Jesus told about a father and son. The son made a mistake, but his father still loved him. Jesus told the story to help people understand that God is like a loving parent. God always loves us, even when we make mistakes. God cares about each one of us.

Sing the song printed below to the tune of "Hot Cross Buns."

God Loves Us
(Tune: "Hot Cross Buns")

God loves us.
God loves us.
Even when we make mistakes, God
still loves us.

Supplies

Reproducible 13A, scissors, scrap paper, glue, box with open top or paper grocery bag, optional: plain paper to wrap box

Feed the Pigs

Photocopy and cut apart the pig cards **(Reproducible 13A)**. Let the children decorate the pigs with crayons.

If you use a box that has writing on the outside, cover the box with plain paper. Leave the top of the box open. If you use a paper bag with writing on the outside, turn the bag inside out. Show the children the box or paper grocery bag.

Say: We're going to pretend this box or bag is a pigpen.

Encourage the children to glue the pig cards all around the box or paper bag. Set the box or bag in an open area of the room. Give the children scrap paper. Have the children crumple the paper into balls.

Say: Our Bible story today is a story Jesus told about a father and son. The son made a mistake and left home. Because of his mistake, the son had to take a job feeding pigs. This made the son very sad. Finally, the son decided to go home and tell his father he was sorry. The father was very happy to see the son. He loved and forgave the son. God always loves us, even when we make mistakes. Let's pretend these paper balls are food for the pigs. Let's feed the pigs.

Have the children take turns tossing the paper balls into the box or bag. After each child's turn, say the child's name and the Bible verse: *(Child's name)*, **"God cares for you"** (1 Peter 5:7, CEV).

Oops!

Supplies

None

Say: Everyone makes mistakes. Listen to this story about a boy named Patrick. When Patrick makes a mistake and does something wrong, shout "Oops!" Then let's think of the right thing for Patrick to do.

One sunny day, Patrick took a walk down the street. He was whistling and wore a happy smile. Patrick was munching on a candy bar. "Mmmm, that was good," he said as he threw the wrapper the sidewalk. *(Oops!)*

Patrick started running down the street. He passed Maria, who was sitting on the sidewalk tying her shoe. He knocked her over and kept on going. *(Oops!)*

Patrick decided to take a short-cut back home. He skipped across down on Mrs. Thompson's yard and trampled her flowers. *(Oops!)*

Adapted from Patrick's Walk, written by Irene Dillard, © 1994 Cokesbury.

After telling the story, **say: When we make a mistake, we can say we're sorry. We can try to do better.**

> ## God loves us, even when we make mistakes.

Parable Prayers

Supplies

construction paper, scissors

Cut out a large heart from construction paper.

Have the children sit in a circle. Show the children the heart.

Say: We know God always loves us, even when we make mistakes. Let's say a thank-you prayer to God.

Give the first child in the circle the heart.

Pray: Thank you, God, for loving *(child's name)* **and** *(her or his)* **friend,** *(name of child sitting next to first child named)*. **Amen.**

Have the child holding the heart repeat the prayer for the friend: **Thank you, God, for** *(name of child sitting next to him or her)*.

Have the child pass the heart to the next child. Repeat until every child has had a turn passing the heart and praying.

REPRODUCIBLE 13A

REPRODUCIBLE 13B

All-in-One
BIBLE FUN

Are you

- Feeling the budget pinch in your children's ministry?
- Unsure of the number of children you'll have in Sunday school each week?
- Working with a Sunday school program that doesn't meet each week?

LET THE FUN BEGIN

Order Today!

Preschool

Elementary

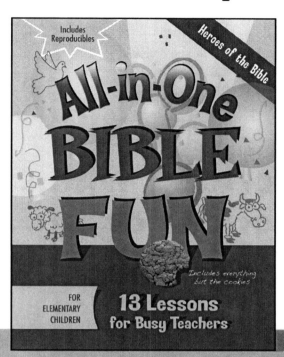

All-in-One Bible Fun

is available for preschool and elementary-age children. Each book will focus on a specific theme:

- *Stories of Jesus*
- *Favorite Bible Stories*
- *Fruit of the Spirit*
- *Heroes of the Bible*

- Thirteen complete lessons in each book

- No additional components to purchase

- Each book includes lesson plans with your choice of arrival activities, a Bible story, a Bible verse and prayer, and games and crafts

- Material is undated so teachers can use the books throughout the year

All-in-One Bible Fun: 13 Lessons for Busy Teachers

Stories of Jesus—Preschool 978-1-426-70778-0
Stories of Jesus—Elementary 978-1-426-70779-7

Favorite Bible Stories—Preschool 978-1-426-70783-4
Favorite Bible Stories—Elementary 978-1-426-70780-3

Fruit of the Spirit—Preschool 978-1-426-70785-8
Fruit of the Spirit—Elementary 978-1-426-70782-7

Heroes of the Bible—Preschool 978-1-426-70784-1
Heroes of the Bible—Elementary 978-1-426-70781-0

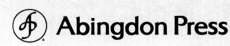

abingdonpress.com | 800-251-3320

One Room SUNDAY SCHOOL®

Working with a broader age group?

One Room Sunday School is designed specifically for a program where four or more age groups are taught in one classroom.

For children age 3 through middle school!

Students will grow together through comprehensive Bible study, application of Bible lessons to everyday discipleship, and a variety of age-appropriate activities.

Abingdon Press

Live B.I.G.'s
One Big Room

A Proven Sunday School Program for Mixed-Age Group Children's Ministries

kit includes everything you need for the quarter

- 3 DVDs
- One Music CD
- One Leader Book

For children age 3 through middle school!

Abingdon Press

CPSIA information can be obtained at www.ICGtesting.com
Printed in the USA
LVOW09s0715180913

352709LV00001B/2/P